GoodFood
Superhealthy
suppers

10 9 8 7 6 5 4 3 2 1

Published in 2012 by BBC Books, an imprint of Ebury Publishing
A Random House Group company

The Random House Group Limited
Reg. No. 954009

Addresses for companies within the Random House Group can be found at www.randomhouse.co.uk

A CIP catalogue record for this book is available from the British Library

The Random House Group Limited supports The Forest Stewardship Council® (FSC®), the
leading international forest certification organisation. Our books carrying the FSC label are
printed on FSC® certified paper. FSC is the only forest certification scheme endorsed by
the leading environmental organisations, including Greenpeace. Our paper procurement
policy can be found at www.randomhouse.co.uk/environment

To buy books by your favourite authors and register for offers visit www.randomhouse.co.uk

Printed and bound by Firmengruppe APPL, aprinta druck, Wemding, Germany
Colour origination by Dot Gradations Ltd, UK

Commissioning Editor: Muna Reyal
Project Editor: Joe Cottington
Designer: Kathryn Gammon
Production: Phil Spencer
Picture Researcher: Gabby Harrington

ISBN: 9781849904711

MIX
Paper from
responsible sources
FSC™ C004592

Picture credits

BBC *Good Food* magazine and BBC Books would like to thank the following people for providing photos. While every effort has
been made to trace and acknowledge all photographers, we should like to apologies should there be any errors or omissions.

Carolyn Barber p141; Peter Cassidy p17, p85, p99, p137, p167, p195; Jean Cazals p173; Will Heap p31, p39, p45, p51, p63, p67, p69,
p103, p109, p111, p113, p115, p117, p119, p143, p147, p153, p159, p165, p171, p210; Amanda Heywood p49, p151, p155, p169;
Sian Irvine p57, p87, p133, p145; David Loftus p33, p157; Gareth Morgans p11, p47, p95, p97, p101, p105, p179, p197, p199; David
Munns p19, p35, p53, p59, p61, p65, p91, p107, p131, p135, p183, p193, p201, p203; Myles New p25, p27, p73, p75, p83, p89, p139,
p187, p205, p207; Stuart Ovenden p29, p79, p175; Lis Parsons p13, p15, p23, p55, p71, p93, p121, p149, p163, p181, p189, p209;
Charlie Richards p43, p81; Maja Smend p21, p161, p191; Roger Stowell p77, p185; Philip Webb p37, p41, p177; Isobel Wield p123,
p125, p127, p129

All the recipes in this book were created by the editorial team at *Good Food* and by regular contributors to BBC magazines.

healthy GoodFood
Superhealthy suppers

Editor **Sharon Brown**

BOOKS

Contents

Introduction

Eating healthily doesn't mean a diet of boring salads and unexciting bland food – healthy food can taste fabulous, is easy to cook and can even save you money. On top of this, making simple changes to our diet can improve our everyday wellbeing and help to prevent serious illnesses. For example, we know that eating less saturated fat will cut our risk of heart disease, and reducing our salt intake can help lower blood pressure and the risk of heart disease and strokes.

When *Good Food* magazine launched the 'superhealthy' label for some of our good-for-you recipes, we worked with a qualified nutritionist to decide that each superhealthy recipe should be:

• low in saturated fat (5g or less per portion)
• low in salt (1.5g or less)
• contain at least one of the following: one-third or more of your daily requirement of fibre, iron, calcium, folic acid and/or vitamin C, or at least one portion of 5-a-day fruit and veg.

Dip into the Midweek Mains chapter and you'll find tempting *Indian spiced shepherd's pie* and *Chicken & chorizo jambalaya*. Extra special ideas – *Venison steak with port sauce* and *Pan-fried salmon with watercress & polenta croûtons* are in Meals to Impress. And we haven't forgotten puds – *Chocolate baked bananas* and *Apple pie samosas* may not sound healthy but they are!

All the ideas here have been tried and tested in the *Good Food* kitchen so you know they'll work, and with each recipe accompanied by a full nutritional breakdown you know they're good for you too.

Sharon

Sharon Brown

Notes and conversion tables

NOTES ON THE RECIPES
- Eggs are large in the UK and Australia and extra large in America unless stated otherwise.
- Wash fresh produce before preparation.
- Recipes contain nutritional analyses for 'sugar', which means the total sugar content including all natural sugars in the ingredients, unless otherwise stated.

OVEN TEMPERATURES

Gas	°C	°C Fan	°F	Oven temp.
¼	110	90	225	Very cool
½	120	100	250	Very cool
1	140	120	275	Cool or slow
2	150	130	300	Cool or slow
3	160	140	325	Warm
4	180	160	350	Moderate
5	190	170	375	Moderately hot
6	200	180	400	Fairly hot
7	220	200	425	Hot
8	230	210	450	Very hot
9	240	220	475	Very hot

APPROXIMATE WEIGHT CONVERSIONS
- All the recipes in this book list both imperial and metric measurements. Conversions are approximate and have been rounded up or down. Follow one set of measurements only; do not mix the two.
- Cup measurements, which are used by cooks in Australia and America, have not been listed here as they vary from ingredient to ingredient. Kitchen scales should be used to measure dry/solid ingredients.

Good Food is concerned about sustainable sourcing and animal welfare. Where possible humanely reared meats, sustainably caught fish (see fishonline. org for further information from the Marine Conservation Society) and free-range chickens and eggs are used when recipes are originally tested.

SPOON MEASURES

Spoon measurements are level unless otherwise specified.

• 1 teaspoon (tsp) = 5ml

• 1 tablespoon (tbsp) = 15ml

• 1 Australian tablespoon = 20ml (cooks in Australia should measure 3 teaspoons where 1 tablespoon is specified in a recipe)

APPROXIMATE LIQUID CONVERSIONS

metric	imperial	AUS	US
50ml	2fl oz	¼ cup	¼ cup
125ml	4fl oz	½ cup	½ cup
175ml	6fl oz	¾ cup	¾ cup
225ml	8fl oz	1 cup	1 cup
300ml	10fl oz/½ pint	½ pint	1¼ cups
450ml	16fl oz	2 cups	2 cups/1 pint
600ml	20fl oz/1 pint	1 pint	2½ cups
1 litre	35fl oz/1¾ pints	1¾ pints	1 quart

Courgette, pea & pesto soup

If you find it a challenge to eat your 5-a-day, try this simple soup, which includes three portions of veg. Pop in a flask to take to work or school.

TAKES 25 MINUTES ● SERVES 4

1 tbsp olive oil

1 garlic clove, sliced

500g/1lb 2oz courgettes, quartered lengthways and chopped

200g/7oz frozen peas

400g can cannellini beans, drained and rinsed

1 litre/1¾ pints hot vegetable stock

2 tbsp basil pesto

1 Heat the oil in a large pan. Cook the garlic for a few seconds, then add the courgettes and cook for 3 minutes until they start to soften. Stir in the peas and cannellini beans, pour on the hot stock and cook for a further 3 minutes.

2 Stir the pesto through the soup with some seasoning, then ladle into bowls and serve with crusty brown bread, if you like.

PER SERVING 200 kcals, protein 12g, carbs 21g, fat 8g, sat fat 2g, fibre 8g, sugar 7g, salt 1.05g

Salmon noodle soup

A new soup idea tinged with Eastern flavours. It's low fat, heart healthy and a good source of omega-3 – plus it tastes truly sensational!

TAKES 35 MINUTES • SERVES 4

1 litre/1¾ pints low-salt chicken stock
2 tsp Thai red curry paste
100g/4oz flat rice noodles
150g pack shiitake mushrooms, sliced
125g pack baby corn, sliced
2 skinless salmon fillets, sliced
juice of 2 limes
1 tbsp reduced-salt soy sauce
pinch of brown sugar
small bunch of coriander, chopped

1 Pour the stock into a large pan, bring to the boil, then stir in the curry paste. Add the noodles and cook for 8 minutes. Tip in the mushrooms and corn, and cook for 2 minutes more.

2 Add the salmon to the pan and cook for 3 minutes or until cooked through. Remove from the heat and stir in the lime juice, soy sauce and a pinch of sugar. Ladle into four bowls and sprinkle over the coriander just before serving.

PER SERVING 265 kcals, protein 19g, carbs 27g, fat 10g, sat fat 2g, fibre 1g, sugar 4g, salt 0.83g

Pistou soup

The pesto and beans can be prepared a day in advance and kept covered with cling film in the fridge. This high-fibre soup delivers two of your 5-a-day.

TAKES 45 MINUTES • SERVES 8

2 tbsp olive oil

1 onion, finely chopped

2 carrots, peeled and finely chopped

2 celery sticks, finely chopped

1 small fennel bulb, trimmed and finely chopped

250g/9oz each turnip, celeriac and parsnip, peeled and finely chopped

140g/5oz frozen peas

140g/5oz canned haricot beans, drained and rinsed

grated Parmesan and croûtons, to serve

FOR THE PESTO

large bunch of basil

1 garlic clove

100ml/3½fl oz extra virgin olive oil

1 Heat the oil in a large pan and sweat the onion, carrots, celery, fennel, turnip, celeriac and parsnip for 5–10 minutes. Pour over 1.6 litres/2¾ pints boiling water, season and simmer for 10–15 minutes, until the vegetables are tender. At the last moment, add the peas and the beans and cook for a further 1 minute. Taste and check the seasoning.

2 Meanwhile, make the pesto sauce. Blanch the basil leaves in boiling water for 5 seconds, then remove and cool under cold running water. Pat dry and purée all the pesto ingredients in a liquidiser. Taste and season, then reserve. Keep in the fridge until required.

3 When ready to serve, pour the soup into a large, warmed tureen and top with some of the pesto sauce. Put Parmesan and croûtons on the table so everyone can help themselves.

PER SERVING 201 kcals, protein 4g, carbs 13g, fat 15g, sat fat 2g, fibre 7g, sugar 7g, salt 0.15g

Indian winter soup

On winter days there's nothing better than warming your hands around a bowl of spicy soup, and this one is packed with four of your 5-a-day.

TAKES 45 MINUTES • SERVES 4–6

100g/4oz pearl barley
2 tbsp vegetable oil
½ tsp brown mustard seeds
1 tsp cumin seeds
2 green chillies, deseeded and finely chopped
1 bay leaf
2 cloves
1 small cinnamon stick
½ tsp ground turmeric
1 large onion, chopped
2 garlic cloves, finely chopped
1 parsnip, cut into chunks
200g/7oz butternut squash, cut into chunks
200g/7oz sweet potato, cut into chunks
1 tsp paprika
1 tsp ground coriander
225g/8oz red split lentils
2 tomatoes, chopped
small bunch of coriander, chopped
1 tsp grated ginger
1 tsp lemon juice

1 Rinse the pearl barley and cook according to the pack instructions. When it is tender, drain and set aside. Meanwhile, heat the oil in a deep, heavy-bottomed pan. Fry the mustard seeds, cumin seeds, chillies, bay leaf, cloves, cinnamon and turmeric until fragrant and the seeds start to crackle. Tip in the onion and garlic, then cook for 5–8 minutes until soft. Stir in the parsnip, squash and sweet potato, and mix thoroughly, making sure the vegetables are fully coated with the oil and spices. Sprinkle in the paprika, ground coriander and seasoning, and stir again.

2 Add the lentils, pearl barley, tomatoes and 1.75 litres/3 pints water. Bring to the boil then turn down and simmer until the vegetables are tender. When the lentils are almost cooked, stir in the chopped coriander, ginger and lemon juice. Serve in warmed bowls.

PER SERVING (4) 445 kcals, protein 19g, carbs 80g, fat 8g, sat fat 1g, fibre 8g, sugar 13g, salt 0.14g

Green cucumber & mint gazpacho

This cool, refreshing soup makes a welcome light lunch on a hot summer's day and it provides four of your 5-a-day. If you like a spicy kick, add more Tabasco to taste.

TAKES 20 MINUTES, PLUS CHILLING
- **SERVES 2**

1 cucumber, halved lengthways, deseeded and roughly chopped
1 yellow pepper, deseeded and roughly chopped
2 garlic cloves, crushed
1 small avocado, chopped
bunch of spring onions, chopped
small bunch of mint, chopped
150g pot fat-free natural yogurt
2 tbsp white wine vinegar
few shakes green Tabasco sauce
snipped chives, to garnish

1 In a food processor or blender, blitz all the ingredients except the chives, reserving half the mint and yogurt, until smooth. Add a little extra vinegar, Tabasco and seasoning to taste, then add a splash of water if you like a slightly thinner soup.

2 Chill until very cold, then serve with a dollop more yogurt, a sprinkling of mint and chive leaves, and a few ice cubes, if you like. The soup will keep in the fridge for 2 days – just give it a stir before you serve.

PER SERVING 186 kcals, protein 8g, carbs 15g, fat 11g, sat fat 2g, fibre 5g, sugar 14g, salt 0.28g

Courgette, potato & Cheddar soup

If you grow your own, this recipe is a great way of using up a glut of veg. Enjoy half now and freeze the remainder for up to 3 months for another day.

TAKES 30 MINUTES • SERVES 8

500g/1lb 2oz potatoes, unpeeled and
    roughly chopped
2 vegetable stock cubes
1kg/2lb 4oz courgettes, roughly
    chopped
1 bunch spring onions, sliced
100g/4oz extra-mature Cheddar,
    grated, plus a little extra to garnish
good grating fresh nutmeg, plus extra
    to garnish

1 Put the potatoes in a large pan with just enough water to cover them and crumble in the stock cubes. Bring to the boil, then cover and cook for 5 minutes. Add the courgettes, put the lid back on and cook for 5 minutes more. Throw in the spring onions, saving one for the garnish, cover and cook for a final 5 minutes.

2 Take off the heat, then stir in the cheese and season with the nutmeg, salt and pepper. Whizz to a thick soup, adding more hot water until you get the consistency you like. Serve scattered with extra grated Cheddar, sliced spring onions and a grating of nutmeg or pepper.

PER SERVING 131 kcals, protein 7g, carbs 14g, fat 6g, sat fat 3g, fibre 2g, sugar 3g, salt 1.31g

Smashed bean dip

For a packed lunch or snack at home, this dip makes a healthy choice. You can also serve it with bread and carrot sticks for dipping or with a handful of tortilla chips.

TAKES 10 MINUTES ● SERVES 4

400g can cannellini beans, drained
   and rinsed
400g can chickpeas, drained and rinsed
juice of 2 lemons, zest of 1
2 garlic cloves, crushed
2 tsp ground cumin
100ml/3½fl oz Greek yogurt
pumpkin seeds, to sprinkle
celery sticks, to dip

1 Put half of the beans and all of the chickpeas into a food processor with the lemon juice, garlic, cumin and yogurt, then whizz until smooth.
2 Tip in the rest of the beans and pulse once to get a very chunky dip. Stir in the lemon zest and plenty of seasoning, then store in the fridge. Serve sprinkled with pumpkin seeds and with celery sticks for dipping.

PER SERVING 172 kcals, protein 11g, carbs 22g, fat 5g, sat fat 1g, fibre 6g, sugar 3g, salt 1.04g

Red onion & Indian-spiced houmous

Houmous makes a perfect snack or starter, or serve it with warmed pitta breads as a light lunch. This recipe is spiked with gentle spices to make it deliciously different.

TAKES 25 MINUTES • SERVES 2

2 tbsp olive oil

1 red onion, thinly sliced

1 tsp each cumin seeds and coriander seeds

½ tsp fennel seeds

400g can chickpeas, drained and rinsed

juice of ½ lemon

1 tbsp tahini

2 tsp finely chopped coriander

pitta breads, to serve

1 In a non-stick pan, heat 1 tablespoon of the oil, then fry the onion until soft and lightly browned. Remove from the heat and set aside to cool while you prepare the rest of the ingredients.

2 Toast the spices for a couple of minutes on a low heat, then remove from the heat and grind to make a powder. In a food processor, blitz together the chickpeas, lemon juice, tahini, spices, some salt, the coriander and the onion until smooth.

3 Tip into a serving bowl and dress with the remaining olive oil. Warm the pitta breads and serve with the houmous.

PER SERVING 314 kcals, protein 11g, carbs 25g, fat 20g, sat fat 2g, fibre 6g, sugar 4g, salt 0.69g

Warm Mexican bean dip with tortilla chips

Make a batch of this healthy dip and divide it into portions to keep in the freezer. Great for a snack or light lunch and delicious warmed through before serving.

TAKES 30 MINUTES ● SERVES 8

1 onion, chopped
1 tbsp olive oil
1 tsp brown soft sugar
1 tsp wine vinegar
1 tsp Cajun seasoning
400g can mixed beans, drained
    and rinsed
400g can chopped tomatoes with garlic
handful of grated Cheddar
100g bag tortilla chips
1 avocado

1 Fry the onion in the olive oil in a small pan until soft. Add the sugar, wine vinegar and Cajun seasoning, and cook for 1 minute. Add the mixed beans and chopped tomatoes. Simmer for 10–15 minutes until the sauce has thickened, then season.

2 Scatter the cheese over the tortilla chips. Microwave on High for 1 minute until the cheese has melted.

3 Stone, peel and chop the avocado and sprinkle over the warmed dip. Serve the dip with the tortilla chips.

PER SERVING 144 kcals, protein 6g, carbs 16g, fat 7g, sat fat 2g, fibre 3g, sugar 3g, salt 0.76g

Carrot & houmous roll-ups

Keep a pack of wraps in the storecupboard and a quick snack is never far away. This is a good idea for a healthy packed lunch to take to work.

TAKES 10 MINUTES • SERVES 4

4 seeded wraps
200g tub houmous
4 carrots
handful of rocket leaves

1 Lay the wraps on a board and spread with the houmous.
2 Coarsely grate the carrots and scatter on top of the houmous. Finish each wrap with a small handful of rocket leaves. Season to taste, roll up and eat.

PER SERVING 355 kcals, protein 10g, carbs 37g, fat 19g, sat fat 3g, fibre 6g, sugar 8g, salt 1.09g

Spiced Indian potato wraps

Sweet potatoes are packed with goodness – high in fibre, very rich in beta-carotene and a good source of vitamin E. They're good baked whole, boiled or mashed too.

TAKES 55 MINUTES ● SERVES 3

4 sweet potatoes, cut into chunky
    wedges
1 red chilli, deseeded and finely
    chopped
2 tbsp olive oil
2 tsp cumin seeds
1 tbsp garam masala
1 red onion, thinly sliced
juice of 1 lime
2 tsp sugar
6–9 chapatis
150ml/¼ pint natural yogurt
large bunch of coriander, leaves only

1 Heat oven to 200C/180C fan/gas 6. Toss the sweet potatoes in a roasting tin with the chilli, 1 teaspoon of the oil, the cumin seeds, garam masala and plenty of seasoning. Roast for 25–35 minutes, turning the wedges halfway, until tender and golden.

2 Meanwhile, fry the onion in the remaining oil for a few minutes until partly softened. Stir in the lime juice and sugar with some seasoning, then turn off the heat.

3 Warm the chapatis according to the pack instructions, then assemble by adding a couple of wedges of sweet potato to each, followed by a scattering of onions, a dollop of yogurt and a small handful of coriander leaves. Roll up and eat.

PER SERVING 445 kcals, protein 13g, carbs 68g, fat 15g, sat fat 3g, fibre 4g, sugar 20g, salt 0.81g

Warm salad of asparagus, bacon, duck egg & hazelnuts

A perfect combination of complementary flavours. Plunging the eggs into iced water stops a black ring forming round the yolk. Make sure the bacon is properly crisp.

TAKES 50 MINUTES ● SERVES 6

6 rashers smoked streaky bacon
3 duck eggs (or 5 large hen's eggs)
500g/1lb 2oz asparagus, about 30
    medium spears
50g/2oz hazelnuts, toasted and
    crushed

FOR THE DRESSING

3 tbsp hazelnut oil
2 tbsp rapeseed oil
1 tbsp cider vinegar
2 tsp smooth French mustard

1 Heat grill to high and cook the bacon for 5 minutes until crisp, then snip into pieces with scissors. Set aside. Cook the eggs in boiling water for 8 minutes (5 minutes for hen's eggs), drain and plunge into iced water, to cool them as quickly as possible.

2 Make the dressing: whisk all the ingredients together with some seasoning. Prepare the asparagus by snapping off the base of each spear – it'll break at the tender point.

3 Just before serving, put the nuts and bacon into a warm oven. Halve the eggs and season. Bring a pan of salted water to the boil; cook the asparagus for about 5 minutes, until just tender. Drain, then divide among plates. Add the egg halves, sprinkle with nuts and bacon, then drizzle with dressing in a zigzag pattern.

PER SERVING 261 kcals, protein 12g, carbs 2g, fat 23g, sat fat 4g, fibre 2g, sugar 2g, salt 0.80g

Skinny pepper, tomato & ham omelette

Eggs are packed with B vitamins and minerals, such as magnesium, zinc and iron. Using fewer yolks helps to lower the cholesterol level of this tempting omelette.

TAKES 25 MINUTES • SERVES 2

2 whole eggs and 3 egg whites
1 tsp olive oil
1 red pepper, deseeded and finely
  chopped
2 spring onions, white and green parts
  kept separate and finely chopped
few slices wafer-thin extra-lean ham,
  shredded
25g/1oz reduced-fat mature Cheddar,
  grated
wholemeal toast, to serve

1 Mix the eggs and egg whites with some seasoning and set aside. Heat the oil in a medium non-stick frying pan and cook the pepper for 3–4 minutes. Throw in the white parts of the spring onions and cook for 1 minute more. Pour in the eggs and cook over a medium heat until almost completely set.

2 Sprinkle on the ham and cheese, and continue cooking the omelette until just set in the centre, or flash it under a hot grill if you like it more well done. Serve straight from the pan with the green part of the spring onion sprinkled on top and some wholemeal toast.

PER SERVING 206 kcals, protein 21g, carbs 5g, fat 12g, sat fat 3g, fibre 1g, sugar 5g, salt 1.21g

Cauliflower fritters with herby dipping sauce

Using sparkling water makes a light, crisp batter. Try other herbs for the dipping sauce,
such as coriander or basil. This makes a good veggie starter.

TAKES 35 MINUTES ● SERVES 4–6
AS A NIBBLE OR STARTER

1 large cauliflower, cut into small
    florets
sunflower oil, for deep-frying

FOR THE BATTER

85g/3oz plain flour
1 tbsp cornflour
125ml/4fl oz sparkling water
½ tsp coriander seeds, ground

FOR THE DIPPING SAUCE

1 large bunch of flat-leaf parsley, finely
    chopped
1 garlic clove, finely chopped
zest and juice of 1 lemon
1 tbsp small capers
3 tbsp olive oil
sea salt, to serve

1 Whisk the batter ingredients together, then let the it rest while you mix together all the sauce ingredients in a separate bowl. Set aside.

2 Cook the cauliflower in boiling salted water for 2 minutes, then drain and refresh with cold water.

3 Heat about 10cm/4in depth of oil in a high-sided pan. Once the oil is hot, test it with a small bit of bread – if it turns golden in 30 seconds, it's ready.

4 Dip the dry cauliflower into the batter, shake off any excess and put in the hot oil. Fry in batches until golden, about 3 minutes, then remove to a plate lined with kitchen paper. To keep warm, put the florets in a low oven. Once all the cauliflower is fried, season with sea salt and serve with the sauce.

PER SERVING (4) 408 kcals, protein 10g,
carbs 25g, fat 30g, sat fat 4g, fibre 5g, sugar 6g,
salt 0.06g

Spiced pea & potato rolls

Children love these crispy, crunchy spring rolls, and as they are packed with veg, they're a healthy choice for a snack. It is a delicious way of using up leftover veg too.

TAKES 50 MINUTES • SERVES 4

2 tbsp vegetable or sunflower oil
2 onions, finely sliced
300g/10oz potatoes, cut into small
  cubes
1 heaped tbsp curry paste
140g/5oz frozen or fresh peas
4 large sheets filo pastry, cut in half
tomato and onion salad and mango
  chutney, to serve

1 Heat oven to 220C/200C fan/gas 7. Heat half the oil in a non-stick frying pan. Tip in the onions and cook until soft and golden, about 8–10 minutes.

2 Meanwhile, boil the potato cubes for 5 minutes, until tender, then drain. Tip into the onions and fry for 2 minutes. Stir in the curry paste and cook for 2 minutes. Add the peas, plus 1 tablespoon water. Cook for 1 minute, stir and season. Tip into a bowl to cool slightly.

3 Brush half the filo half-sheets with some remaining oil, then lay the remaining sheets on top so you have four double layers. Spoon a quarter of the potato mix along one edge of each, leaving space at each end. Fold in the ends then roll up to seal. Put seam-side down on a baking sheet, brush with the remaining oil and bake for 20 minutes, or until crisp. Serve warm with mango chutney and a tomato and onion salad.

PER SERVING 240 kcals, protein 7g, carbs 37g, fat 8g, sat fat 1g, fibre 4g, sugar 6g, salt 0.46g

Chicken livers on toast

Most often used in pâtés and stuffings, chicken livers are also delicious pan-fried and served on toast as a starter or light lunch. They're great value for money too.

TAKES 30 MINUTES ● SERVES 4

250g/9oz chicken livers
2 shallots, finely chopped
large handful of flat-leaf parsley, leaves very roughly chopped
1 tbsp capers, drained and rinsed, roughly chopped
2 tbsp olive oil
3 tbsp sherry vinegar
4 slices good-quality bread, such as sourdough
1 tbsp plain flour
large pinch of cayenne pepper
sea salt, to serve

1 Pick over the livers, cutting away any fatty bits and sinew, then pat the livers dry. Put the shallots, parsley and capers into a bowl and drizzle with half the olive oil and 1 tablespoon of the vinegar.

2 Toast the bread (preferably on a griddle but a toaster is fine). Toss the livers in the flour and cayenne pepper, and season generously. Heat the rest of the oil in a frying pan and fry the livers over a really high heat for 4–5 minutes until brown and crisp on the outside and cooked, but still a little pink in the middle. Splash the remaining vinegar into the pan and bubble down for 1 minute.

3 Tip the contents of the pan in with the shallot and parsley, toss everything together, season to taste, then pile on to the toasted bread. Season with a little crunchy sea salt and serve.

PER SERVING 221 kcals, protein 14g, carbs 25g, fat 8g, sat fat 1g, fibre 2g, sugar 1g, salt 0.83g

Baked eggs with spinach & tomato

Rich in protein, vitamins and minerals, eggs make a valuable contribution to our diet. They provide choline, which boosts memory, and the yolk is a source of vitamin D.

TAKES 20 MINUTES ● SERVES 4

100g bag spinach leaves
400g can chopped tomatoes
1 tsp chilli flakes
4 eggs
crusty bread, to serve (optional)

1 Heat oven to 200C/180C fan/gas 6. Put the spinach in a colander, then pour over a kettle of boiling water to wilt the leaves. Squeeze out excess water and divide the spinach among four small ovenproof dishes.

2 Mix the tomatoes with the chilli flakes and some seasoning, then add to the dishes with the spinach. Make a small well in the centre of each and crack in an egg. Bake for 12–15 minutes or more, depending on how you like your eggs. Serve with crusty bread, if you like.

PER SERVING 114 kcals, protein 9g, carbs 3g, fat 7g, sat fat 2g, fibre 2g, sugar 2g, salt 0.43g

Tofu & asparagus pad Thai

This good-for-you supper is suitable for vegans. If asparagus isn't in season, you can use broccoli florets; if you prefer, add extra lime juice to replace the tamarind.

TAKES 30 MINUTES • SERVES 4

200g/7oz flat rice noodles
2 limes, 1 juiced, 1 cut into wedges
1 tbsp tamarind paste
2 tbsp sweet chilli sauce, plus extra for serving
2 tbsp vegetable or sunflower oil
300g/10oz firm tofu, drained, patted dry and cut into cubes
10 asparagus spears, trimmed and sliced on the diagonal
6 spring onions, halved and thinly sliced lengthways
300g bag beansprouts
3 garlic cloves, finely chopped
handful each of coriander leaves and salted peanuts, to garnish

1 Cook the noodles according to the pack instructions, then drain and set aside. Mix the lime juice, tamarind and chilli sauce in a small bowl. Set aside.
2 Heat 1 tablespoon of the oil in a non-stick frying pan or wok and fry the tofu for 5–8 minutes, until golden all over. Set aside.
3 Add the remaining oil to the pan and stir-fry the asparagus until tender. Tip in the spring onions, beansprouts and garlic. Cook for 2 minutes more. Stir in the drained noodles, lime sauce and some salt. Mix in the tofu and heat through. Serve with coriander and salted peanuts for sprinkling over and lime wedges alongside.

PER SERVING 321 kcals, protein 12g, carbs 53g, fat 8g, sat fat 1g, fibre 3g, sugar 8g, salt 0.74g

Chickpea & coriander burgers

A healthy, low-fat, high-fibre veggie alternative to the classic burger. The recipe can easily be doubled and the burgers can be frozen uncooked or cooked.

TAKES 30 MINUTES • SERVES 4

400g can chickpeas, drained and rinsed
zest of 1 lemon, plus juice ½
1 tsp ground cumin
small bunch of coriander, half chopped
1 egg
100g/4oz fresh breadcrumbs
1 medium red onion, ½ diced, ½ sliced
1 tbsp olive oil
4 small wholemeal buns

TO SERVE

1 large tomato, sliced
½ cucumber, sliced
chilli sauce

1 In a food processor, whizz the chickpeas, lemon zest and juice, cumin, the chopped coriander, the egg and some seasoning. Scrape into a bowl and mix with 85g/3oz of the breadcrumbs and the diced onions. Form the mixture into four burgers, press the remaining breadcrumbs on to both sides and chill.

2 Heat the oil in a frying pan until hot. Fry the burgers for 4 minutes on each side, keeping the heat on medium so they don't burn. To serve, slice each bun and fill with a burger, some sliced onion, tomato and cucumber, a dollop of chilli sauce and the remaining coriander.

PER SERVING 344 kcals, protein 15g, carbs 56g, fat 8g, sat fat 1g, fibre 6g, sugar 6g, salt 1.30g

Mustard-glazed pork with apple Caesar salad

The crunchy apple and creamy dressing on the salad make a perfect accompaniment to the mustardy pork – and all in less than half an hour.

TAKES 25 MINUTES ● SERVES 4

4 lean pork escalopes or loin steaks, trimmed of any fat
1 tbsp Dijon mustard
1 tbsp extra virgin olive oil
juice of ¼ lemon
1 tsp Worcestershire sauce
3 tbsp low-fat natural yogurt
50g/2oz Parmesan, finely grated
2 apples, unpeeled, cored and thinly sliced
2 baby romaine lettuce (about 300g/10oz), leaves separated and large ones roughly torn

1 Brush the pork with 2 teaspoons of the mustard and set aside. In a large serving bowl, mix all the remaining ingredients, except the lettuce, with some seasoning. Top with the lettuce leaves but don't mix together yet.

2 Griddle or grill the pork for 3–4 minutes on each side, until cooked through and golden, then allow to rest for 1 minute. Slice the pork then toss with the salad and dressing, combining everything well.

PER SERVING 283 kcals, protein 34g, carbs 10g, fat 12g, sat fat 4g, fibre 2g, sugar 10g, salt 0.79g

Spaghetti with sardines

Using sardines in this super-quick dish makes a great, sustainable alternative to anchovies – they're also cheaper and a great source of omega-3.

TAKES 20 MINUTES • SERVES 4

400g/14oz spaghetti
1 tbsp olive oil
2 garlic cloves, crushed
pinch of chilli flakes
227g can chopped tomatoes
2 × 95g cans skinless boneless
    sardines in tomato sauce
100g/4oz pitted black olives, roughly
    chopped
1 tbsp capers, drained
small handful of parsley, chopped

1 Cook the spaghetti in a large pan of boiling salted water according to the pack instructions. Meanwhile, make the sauce. Heat the oil in a medium pan and cook the garlic for 1 minute. Add the chilli flakes, tomatoes and sardines, breaking up roughly with a wooden spoon. Heat for 2–3 minutes, then stir in the olives, capers and most of the parsley. Mix well to combine.
2 Drain the pasta, reserving a couple of tablespoons of the water. Add the pasta to the sauce and mix well, adding the reserved water if the sauce is a little thick. Divide among four bowls and sprinkle with the remaining parsley.

PER SERVING 495 kcals, protein 21g, carbs 77g, fat 14g, sat fat 2g, fibre 5g, sugar 5g, salt 1.07g

Prawn, dill & cucumber pasta salad

The fennel and dill combine to add a fabulous flavour to this salad. Keep it cool and take it to a picnic or make it for a take-to-work lunch.

TAKES ABOUT 20 MINUTES
● **SERVES 4–6**

300g/10oz pasta shapes
small bunch of dill, chopped
juice of ½ lemon
5 tbsp half-fat soured cream
300g/10oz cooked peeled prawns
1 cucumber, diced
1 fennel bulb, shredded

1 Cook the pasta in a large pan of boiling salted water according to the pack instructions, drain and cool under running water.
2 Tip the pasta into a bowl and toss with the dill, lemon juice and soured cream. Stir through the prawns, cucumber and fennel. Season and serve.

PER SERVING (4) 370 kcals, protein 28g, carbs 60g, fat 4g, sat fat 1g, fibre 4g, sugar 5g, salt 1.41g

Glazed salmon with green bean & bulghar salad

To make sure the cooked green beans retain their colour, rinse just drained beans quickly under cold running water to stop the cooking process.

TAKES 25 MINUTES ● SERVES 2

140g/5oz bulghar wheat
1 tbsp olive oil
2 skinless salmon fillets
6 spring onions, sliced
juice and zest of ½ lemon
1 tbsp clear honey
juice of 1 orange, plus 1 tsp zest
200g/7oz trimmed fine green beans

1 Cook the bulghar wheat according to the pack instructions. Heat the olive oil in a frying pan over a medium heat. Add the salmon fillets and cook for 3 minutes on each side. Stir in the spring onions and cook for 1 minute. Add the lemon juice, honey, orange juice and zest to the pan and bubble for 1 minute more to make a sauce.

2 Meanwhile, boil the green beans for 4 minutes or until tender. Drain. Stir the bulghar wheat with a fork, mixing in the green beans, lemon zest and a little of the sauce. Serve the salmon on a bed of bulghar and beans, with the rest of the sauce spooned over.

PER SERVING 603 kcals, protein 38g, carbs 66g, fat 23g, sat fat 4g, fibre 3g, sugar 13g, salt 0.18g

Thai turkey stir-fry

You can add other favourites to this quickly made stir-fry, such as red pepper strips, carrot sticks or baby corn. Taste, then add more chilli powder if you like a fiery kick.

TAKES 25 MINUTES • SERVES 4

300g/10oz rice noodles
1 tsp sunflower oil
400g/14oz turkey breast, cut into thin strips and any fat removed
350g/12oz green beans, trimmed and halved
1 red onion, sliced
2 garlic cloves, sliced
juice of 1 lime, plus extra wedges for serving
1 tsp chilli powder
1 red chilli, deseeded and finely chopped
1 tbsp fish sauce
handful of mint, roughly chopped
handful of coriander, roughly chopped

1 Cook the rice noodles according to the pack instructions. Heat the oil in a non-stick pan and fry the turkey over a high heat for 2 minutes. Add the beans, onion and garlic, and cook for a further 5 minutes.

2 Stir in the lime juice, chilli powder, fresh chilli and fish sauce, then cook for 3 minutes more. Stir in the noodles and herbs, then toss everything together before serving.

PER SERVING 425 kcals, protein 32g, carbs 71g, fat 3g, sat fat 1g, fibre 4g, sugar 4g, salt 0.92g

Sticky pork & radish noodles

For a change, you can use 250g/9oz shredded cooked chicken for this dish. Whisk the lime juice and honey together to make a dressing, and stir through the chicken.

TAKES 30 MINUTES • SERVES 4

3 tbsp clear honey
zest and juice of 2 limes
450g/1lb pork fillet, thinly sliced
200g/7oz medium egg noodles
140g/5oz radishes, thinly sliced
200g/7oz mangetout, cut into strips
1 large carrot, cut into matchsticks
small bunch of coriander, roughly
   chopped
2 tbsp sunflower oil

1 Whisk the honey and lime zest and juice together in a large bowl and season. Add the pork and mix well to coat in the marinade. Cover and chill for 10 minutes.

2 Cook the noodles in a pan of boiling water for 4 minutes. Mix together the radishes, mangetout, carrot and coriander in a serving bowl. Heat the oil in a large non-stick frying pan. Remove the pork from the marinade and add to the pan, reserving the marinade. Stir-fry for 3–5 minutes, until golden and cooked through. Add the reserved marinade to the pan and allow to bubble for 1 minute.

3 Drain the noodles and divide them among serving plates. Spoon the pork and all the pan juices over the vegetables and gently mix. Serve the noodles with the pork and vegetables.

PER SERVING 280 kcals, protein 27g, carbs 14g, fat 13g, sat fat 3g, fibre 2g, sugar 13g, salt 0.19g

Moroccan chicken with lemon couscous

For a change from pasta or rice, couscous is always a popular accompaniment for midweek family meals. It's just right with this delicious chicken dish.

TAKES 30 MINUTES • SERVES 4

250g/9oz couscous
zest and juice 1 of lemon
4 skinless boneless chicken breasts,
    sliced into large strips
1 tsp olive oil
1 tbsp clear honey
1 tsp ground cinnamon
1 tsp ground cumin
400g can chopped tomatoes
150ml/¼ pint chicken stock
200g/7oz fine green beans, trimmed

1 Put the couscous, half the lemon zest and half the juice in a medium bowl and pour over 400ml/14fl oz boiling water. Cover with cling film and leave to soak while you cook the chicken.

2 Heat the oil in a large non-stick frying pan, drizzle the honey and some seasoning over the chicken and fry over a medium heat for 5–6 minutes, until the chicken is golden.

3 Mix in the spices, followed by the tomatoes, stock, beans and remaining lemon zest and juice. Bring to the boil and simmer, uncovered, for 8–10 minutes or until the beans are tender. Fork through the couscous to fluff it up, then serve with the chicken.

PER SERVING 344 kcals, protein 41g, carbs 39g, fat 4g, sat fat 1g, fibre 2g, sugar 6g, salt 0.44g

Courgette, broccoli & gremolata pasta

The light flavours of this dish make it just right for a summer evening. Pack up any leftovers for a tempting next-day packed lunch.

TAKES 30 MINUTES ● SERVES 4

2 garlic cloves, finely grated
zest of 2 lemons, plus a squeeze of
    juice
small bunch of parsley, finely chopped
200g/7oz broccoli, broken into florets
400g/14oz pasta bows or other shapes
1 tsp olive oil
2 courgettes, chopped

1 To make the gremolata, mix the garlic, lemon zest and juice in a small bowl with the parsley and some seasoning.
2 Bring a large pan of salted water to the boil, add the broccoli and cook for 2–3 minutes until just tender. Use a slotted spoon to remove, then set aside. Bring the water back to the boil, add the pasta and cook according to the pack instructions.
3 Heat the olive oil in a frying pan, add the courgettes and cook over a high heat for 3–4 minutes until starting to turn golden, tip in the broccoli and continue to cook for 1 minute until warmed through.
4 Drain the pasta, reserving about 2 tablespoons of the cooking water, then add the pasta, cooking water and gremolata to the vegetables. Mix well and serve.

PER SERVING 390 kcals, protein 16g, carbs 79g, fat 4g, sat fat 1g, fibre 5g, sugar 4g, salt 0.04g

Skewered sardines with tartare dressing

The sardines are scrumptious barbecued, but if the weather lets you down they're just as good drizzled with oil and cooked under the grill.

TAKES 30 MINUTES • SERVES 4

zest and juice of 1 lemon
4 tbsp olive oil
12 sardines, cleaned, gutted and heads cut off (ask your fishmonger to do this for you)
small bunch of dill, finely chopped
small bunch of parsley, finely chopped
1 tbsp capers, drained and chopped
2 tbsp cornichons, drained and finely chopped
8 wooden skewers, soaked in water

1 Pour half the lemon juice and 1 tablespoon of the olive oil over the sardines, then rub them both into the fish's cavity and skin. Lay 2–3 sardines (depending on size) side by side and thread a skewer through the tail ends and another through the head ends, packing the fish closely together.

2 To make the tartare dressing, combine the lemon zest and the rest of the juice and oil with the dill, parsley, capers, cornichons and some seasoning. Set aside.

3 Season the sardines really well, then carefully lift them on to a hot barbecue. Cook for 3–4 minutes on each side, gently turning the skewers, then transfer to a serving plate. Spoon over a little dressing and serve the rest on the side.

PER SERVING 400 kcals, protein 37g, carbs 1g, fat 28g, sat fat 5g, fibre none, sugar none, salt 0.91g

Superhealthy Singapore noodles

The wonderful prawn-and-chicken combination make this easy stir-fry a special favourite with children. Add more or less curry paste according to your taste.

TAKES 30 MINUTES • SERVES 4

3 nests medium egg noodles
2 tbsp sunflower oil
100g/4oz Tenderstem broccoli, stems sliced at an angle
1 red pepper, deseeded, quartered and cut into strips
85g/3oz baby corn, quartered lengthways
2 garlic cloves, shredded
1 red chilli, deseeded and chopped
thumb-size piece ginger, peeled and finely chopped
2 skinless chicken breasts, sliced
100g/4oz shelled raw king prawns
1 heaped tbsp Madras curry paste
2 tsp soy sauce
100g/4oz beansprouts
15g pack coriander, chopped
4 spring onions, shredded
lime wedges, for squeezing

1 Pour boiling water over the noodles and leave to soften. Meanwhile, heat half the oil in a large non-stick wok and stir-fry all the vegetables, except the beansprouts, onions and spring onions, with the garlic, chilli and ginger until softened. If the broccoli won't soften, add a splash of water to the wok and cover to create some steam.

2 Tip the veg on to a plate, add the rest of the oil to the wok then briefly stir-fry the chicken and prawns until just cooked. Set aside with the vegetables and add the curry paste to the pan. Stir-fry for a few seconds then add 150ml/¼ pint water and the soy sauce. Allow to bubble then add the drained, softened noodles and the beansprouts, and toss together to coat.

3 Return the vegetables, chicken and prawns to the wok with the coriander and spring onions. Toss well and serve with lime wedges.

PER SERVING 362 kcals, protein 40g, carbs 33g, fat 9g, sat fat 1g, fibre 6g, sugar 5g, salt 1.39g

Spaghetti with walnuts, raisins & parsley

This is a great recipe to make from the storecupboard and a good way of using up leftover dried fruit and nuts. Another plus is that it won't break the budget!

TAKES 25 MINUTES • SERVES 4

300g/10oz spaghetti
2 tbsp olive oil
2 onions, sliced
5 tbsp raisins or sultanas
250ml/9fl oz chicken or vegetable stock
50g/2oz Parmesan, grated
5 tbsp chopped walnuts
small bunch of flat-leaf parsley, finely chopped

1 Cook the pasta in boiling water, according to the pack instructions. Meanwhile, heat the oil in a frying pan and cook the onions until soft and golden brown – about 8–10 minutes.
2 Add the raisins or sultanas and stock, and cook for 2–3 minutes until heated through. Toss with the pasta, Parmesan, walnuts and parsley, and serve.

PER SERVING 526 kcals, protein 18g, carbs 74g, fat 19g, sat fat 4g, fibre 4g, sugar 19g, salt 0.44g

Moroccan-style chicken stew

This quick-cook stew is made in one pot, is low in fat and counts as two of your 5-a-day, too. Ras-el-hanout is a blend of spicy, herbal and floral flavours.

TAKES 30 MINUTES • SERVES 4

1 tbsp olive oil
1 onion, chopped
1 garlic clove, crushed
1 tbsp ras-el-hanout or Moroccan
  spice mix
4 boneless skinless chicken breasts,
  sliced
300ml/½ pint reduced-salt chicken
  stock
400g can chickpeas, drained and rinsed
12 dried apricots, sliced
small bunch of coriander, chopped

1 Heat the oil in a large, shallow pan and cook the onion for 3 minutes. Add the garlic and spice mix and cook for a further minute.

2 Tip in the chicken and cook for around 3 minutes, then pour in the stock, chickpeas and apricots. Simmer for 5 minutes or until the chicken is cooked through. Stir through the coriander and serve immediately with couscous and a green salad, if you like.

PER SERVING 309 kcals, protein 40g, carbs 24g, fat 6g, sat fat 1g, fibre 5g, sugar 13g, salt 0.66g

Harissa lamb & pepper kebabs

To make a veggie version of this spicy and fragrant dish, swap the lamb cubes for chunks of halloumi. A 250g/9oz block will give 16 chunks, enough for two per skewer.

TAKES 25 MINUTES • SERVES 4

2 tbsp harissa paste
1 tbsp olive oil
400g/14oz lamb steaks, trimmed of any fat and chopped into chunks
2 red peppers, deseeded and chopped into large chunks
2 red onions, each cut into 8 wedges through the root so the wedges don't fall apart
250g/9oz couscous, flavoured or plain

1 Heat the grill. In a large bowl, mix the harissa with the oil, then tip in the lamb chunks, peppers and onions. Add some salt and pepper, and toss everything together to coat well.

2 Thread the lamb, peppers and onions evenly on to eight skewers and put on a baking sheet. Scrape any leftover marinade over the skewers.

3 Grill for 8–10 minutes, turning frequently and basting the kebabs with any of the juices that run off. Meanwhile, prepare the couscous according to the pack instructions.

4 Divide the couscous among four plates, top each with a couple of skewers and drizzle over any pan juices.

PER SERVING 351 kcals, protein 25g, carbs 41g, fat 11g, sat fat 3g, fibre 2g, sugar 8g, salt 0.26g

Honey & sesame beef noodles

The combination of honey and sesame is delicious. This recipe is easily halved to serve one or doubled to serve the family. For a bit of a kick, add a few chilli flakes.

TAKES 25 MINUTES • SERVES 2

100g/4oz wholewheat noodles
2 tsp sunflower oil
125g pack purple sprouting broccoli (or Tenderstem), cut into short lengths
100g/4oz sugar snap peas, halved
4 spring onions, cut into short lengths
2 tbsp reduced-salt soy sauce
175g/6oz lean rump steak, thinly sliced
2 tsp sesame seeds
2 tbsp clear honey

1 Cook the noodles in boiling salted water, according to the pack instructions, until tender; drain and rinse in cold water. Heat half the oil in a non-stick wok. Add the broccoli, peas and 2 tablespoons water, then cover and steam-fry for 3 minutes.
2 Remove the lid, add the onions and stir-fry for 2 minutes, adding a splash more water if needed to cook the veg. Add the noodles and half the soy sauce and toss with the veg. Divide between two bowls and keep warm.
3 Wipe out the wok and heat the remaining oil until smoking. Tip in the beef and stir-fry for 2 minutes over a high heat, but don't move it around too much or it will release liquid and stew rather than fry. Tip in the sesame seeds, cook for 1 minute more, then add the honey. Toss to coat the beef well, then add the remaining soy and bubble briefly.
4 Spoon the beef over the vegetables and noodles, and serve immediately.

PER SERVING 420 kcals, protein 32g, carbs 50g, fat 12g, sat fat 3g, fibre 8g, sugar 18g, salt 1.45g

Crunchy detox salad

This salad is full of vibrant colours, textures and flavours. Fabulous for a lunch box or light supper, it will keep in the fridge for up to 3 days. Give it a stir before serving.

TAKES 20 MINUTES • SERVES 4

250g/9oz broccoli, cut into small florets
100g/4oz ready-to-eat dried apricots, cut into strips
300g/10oz red cabbage, finely shredded
400g can chickpeas, drained and rinsed
50g/2oz sunflower seeds
1 small red onion, finely sliced
2cm/¾in piece ginger, grated
juice of 1 small orange
1 tbsp balsamic vinegar
2 tsp olive oil

1 Blanch the broccoli in a pan of boiling water for 1 minute. Drain and quickly cool under cold running water, then pat dry with kitchen paper. Put in a bowl with the apricots, red cabbage, chickpeas and sunflower seeds.
2 Put the onion and ginger in a bowl with the orange juice, vinegar and oil. Mix well. Leave for 5 minutes to soften the onion, then add to the salad and thoroughly toss everything together.

PER SERVING 248 kcals, protein 12g, carbs 28g, fat 11g, sat fat 1g, fibre 9g, sugar 16g, salt 0.38g

Crab & asparagus salad with chilli & lime dressing

This dish would also be perfect as a starter and would easily serve six. Asparagus is rich in folic acid and a good source of soluble fibre.

TAKES 15 MINUTES ● SERVES 4

200g pack asparagus tips
2 large handfuls baby spinach leaves
½ cucumber, cut into ribbons with
    a peeler
100g/4oz white crab meat

FOR THE DRESSING

juice of 1 lime
1 tbsp olive oil
2 tbsp rice wine vinegar
pinch of sugar
1 tsp Thai fish sauce
1 red chilli, deseeded and finely
    chopped

1 Cook the asparagus in plenty of boiling salted water until tender, about 3 minutes, then drain and cool under running water. Set aside on kitchen paper to absorb any excess water.
2 To make the dressing, combine all the ingredients in a small bowl and set aside.
3 On a large platter or four smaller plates, arrange the leaves and cucumber, then scatter on the asparagus and crab meat. Drizzle over the dressing just before serving.

PER SERVING 70 kcals, protein 7g, carbs 3g, fat 4g, sat fat 1g, fibre 1g, sugar 2g, salt 0.59g

Mediterranean sardine salad

This superquick no-cook supper is heart healthy and a good source of omega-3 and calcium. Leftovers can be packed into a baguette for a satisfying take-to-work lunch.

TAKES 15 MINUTES ● SERVES 4

90g bag salad leaves
handful of black olives, roughly
    chopped
1 tbsp capers, drained
2 × 120g cans sardines in tomato
    sauce, drained and sauce reserved
1 tbsp olive oil
1 tbsp red wine vinegar

1 Divide the salad leaves among four plates, then sprinkle over the olives and capers.
2 Roughly break up the sardines and add to the salad. Mix the tomato sauce with the oil and vinegar, and drizzle the dressing over the salad.

PER SERVING 140 kcals, protein 10g, carbs 1g, fat 10g, sat fat 2g, fibre 1g, sugar 1g, salt 0.90g

Chicken & pasta salad

Packed with family favourites, this salad is always a winner. Eat for a summer lunch or supper, or take on a picnic. The chicken can be griddled or barbecued.

TAKES 30 MINUTES • SERVES 4

1 red pepper, deseeded and thickly sliced
1 red onion, thickly sliced
1 tbsp olive oil
300g/10oz penne or fusilli pasta
4 boneless skinless chicken breasts
2 tbsp each chopped thyme and oregano
pinch of dried chilli flakes
2 garlic cloves, crushed
150g pack cherry tomatoes, halved
50g bag rocket leaves
1 tbsp white wine vinegar

1 Heat oven to 220C/200C fan/gas 7. Mix the pepper and onion with 1 teaspoon of the oil and roast for 20 minutes.

2 Cook the pasta according to the pack instructions. Drain and set aside.

3 Meanwhile, put the chicken breasts between two sheets of cling film and bash with a rolling pin until they're about 1cm/½in thick. Mix together the remaining oil, herbs, chilli and garlic then rub all over the chicken. Heat a griddle or barbecue and cook the chicken for 3–4 minutes on each side.

4 Slice the chicken on a board, scrape into the pasta with any juices, plus the roasted onion and pepper, cherry tomatoes, rocket, vinegar and some seasoning. Toss together and eat warm or cold.

PER SERVING 470 kcals, protein 44g, carbs 64g, fat 6g, sat fat 1g, fibre 4g, sugar 7g, salt 0.26g

Vietnamese prawn & noodle salad with crispy shallots

The lime dressing adds a wonderful zing to this simply put together salad. Making the fried shallots is optional, but it is well worth it as they're incredibly delicious.

TAKES 25 MINUTES • SERVES 4

200g/7oz thin rice noodles
200g/7oz large cooked peeled prawns
1 small red onion, halved and sliced
1 small red chilli, seeded and sliced
1 small cucumber, shaved into ribbons (use a peeler)
1 large handful each coriander and mint
2 tbsp roasted peanuts, roughly chopped

FOR THE DRESSING

juice of 3 limes
1 tbsp brown soft sugar
2 tsp fish sauce
1 garlic clove, crushed

FOR THE CRISPY SHALLOTS

vegetable oil, for frying
5 shallots, thinly sliced
flour, for dusting

1 For the crispy shallots, heat 5cm/2in oil in a wok until hot. Toss the shallot slices with flour, shake off the excess and fry in the oil until golden. They fry quickly, about 1 minute. Drain on kitchen paper, sprinkle with salt and set aside.

2 To make the dressing, mix together the lime juice, sugar, fish sauce and garlic, and set aside.

3 In a large mixing bowl, pour boiling water over the noodles. Leave them for 2 minutes or until they are just cooked, then rinse under cold running water. Drain well, shaking the sieve numerous times to remove the excess water, then put back in the bowl.

4 Add the prawns, onion, chilli, cucumber and herbs to the noodles. Pour the dressing over, mix, then sprinkle with the crispy shallots and peanuts and serve straight away.

PER SERVING 331 kcals, protein 18g, carbs 53g, fat 7g, sat fat 1g, fibre 2g, sugar 7g, salt 1.41g

Warm roasted squash & Puy lentil salad

Canned pulses are always a good storecupboard standby, as they're naturally high in protein and are versatile and brilliant for bulking out salads, soups and stews.

TAKES 40 MINUTES ● SERVES 4

1kg/2lb 4oz butternut squash, cut into chunks
1½ tbsp olive oil
1 garlic clove, crushed
2 tsp thyme leaves
1 tbsp balsamic vinegar
1 tsp wholegrain mustard
2 × 400g cans Puy lentils in water, drained and rinsed
½ red onion, sliced
100g bag spinach leaves
150g pack cherry tomatoes, halved
40g/1½oz Cheshire cheese
1–2 tbsp pumpkin seeds, toasted

1 Heat oven to 200C/180C fan/gas 6. Toss the butternut squash in a roasting tin with 1 tablespoon of the oil, the garlic, thyme leaves and seasoning. Roast for 25–30 minutes or until tender.
2 Mix together the balsamic vinegar, remaining oil, mustard and 1–2 tablespoons water. Toss the drained lentils with the dressing, red onion, spinach and cherry tomatoes.
3 Divide the lentil mixture among four plates. Top with the roasted squash, then crumble over the Cheshire cheese and pumpkin seeds, and serve.

PER SERVING 304 kcals, protein 15g, carbs 41g, fat 10g, sat fat 3g, fibre 13g, sugar 15g, salt 0.35g

Clementine, feta & winter leaf salad

This wonderfully light salad is quickly put together and makes a fresh and zingy snack, or could be served as a special-occasion starter.

TAKES 20 MINUTES • SERVES 8

6–8 seedless clementines

2 heads red chicory

100g/4oz watercress

1 fennel bulb, halved, cored and very finely sliced

1 red onion, halved and finely sliced

200g pack feta, cut into cubes

small handful of parsley, finely chopped

FOR THE DRESSING

juice of 1 clementine

juice of 1 lemon

4 tbsp olive oil

1 tsp caster sugar

1 Whisk the dressing ingredients in a jug, season with salt and set aside.

2 To make the salad, peel the clementines and slice whole. In a bowl, gently toss the chicory and watercress with the fennel and onion. Put slices of clementine on opposite sides of each plate, mound a pile of leaves in the middle, then scatter over the feta. Stir the parsley through the dressing and drizzle it over the salad.

PER SERVING 149 kcals, protein 5g, carbs 8g, fat 11g, sat fat 4g, fibre 2g, sugar 7g, salt 0.7g

Steak salad with blue cheese vinaigrette

This salad makes a special supper for two and the dressing adds a fabulous flavour. The steak can either be barbecued, griddled or grilled.

TAKES 25 MINUTES ● SERVES 2

1 fillet or rump steak (about
    300g/10oz), trimmed
140g/5oz green beans, trimmed
1 head red chicory, leaves separated
25g/1oz walnuts, roughly chopped

FOR THE DRESSING

zest and juice of ½ lemon
1 tbsp walnut or olive oil
1 tbsp chopped tarragon
1 small shallot, finely chopped
1 tbsp crumbled blue cheese (we used
    Danish Blue)

1 Season the steak with lots of pepper and a little salt. Cook on the barbecue, on a griddle or under the grill for 2–3 minutes each side for medium–rare, or to your liking. Let sit for 10 minutes, then cut into slices.

2 For the dressing, in a small bowl whisk together the lemon zest, juice, oil, tarragon, shallot, cheese and some salt and pepper.

3 Cook the beans in boiling water until just tender. Drain and rinse under cold water, then drain thoroughly.

4 Divide the chicory leaves between two plates and top with the beans, walnuts and steak slices. Pour the dressing over the salad just before eating.

PER SERVING 390 kcals, protein 38g, carbs 5g, fat 24g, sat fat 5g, fibre 3g, sugar 3g, salt 0.42g

Honeyed sesame chicken with peach & cucumber salad

The chicken breasts are sautéed, finished with a honey glaze and served with a salad that has a honey dressing. Try to buy local honey for a tremendous flavour.

TAKES 35 MINUTES ● SERVES 4

2 tbsp sunflower oil
4 chicken breasts, skin-on and
    preferably corn-fed
2 tbsp good-quality clear honey
2 tsp sesame seeds

FOR THE SALAD

1 small cucumber, peeled and
    deseeded
small piece of red chilli, chopped
zest and juice of 1 large lime
2 ripe peaches
1 tsp good-quality clear honey
3 tbsp olive oil
2 handfuls lamb's lettuce, washed
    and dried

1 Heat oven to 180C/160C fan/gas 4. Heat the sunflower oil in a large frying pan over a medium heat. Season the chicken breasts with a little salt on both sides and sauté, skin-side down. After about 5 minutes, when the skin is brown and crisp, flip the chicken and brown it lightly all over. Transfer to a baking sheet and coat each breast in the honey. Sprinkle with sesame seeds and roast for 10–12 minutes until cooked through.

2 Meanwhile, to make the salad, slice the cucumber and toss in a bowl with the chilli and lime zest. Tip the peaches into another bowl and pour over boiling water, then immediately refresh under a cold tap. Peel, then slice and add to the cucumber and chilli. Mix the lime juice with the honey and oil. Toss with the lamb's lettuce and cucumber salad. Slice the chicken and serve with the salad.

PER SERVING 373 kcals, protein 33g, carbs 12g, fat 22g, sat fat 4g, fibre 2g, sugar 12g, salt 0.18g

Soba noodle & edamame salad with grilled tofu

Edamame (or soy) beans can be bought fresh or frozen and are packed with nutrients. They have a slightly nutty taste. You can use broad beans instead, if you prefer.

TAKES 30 MINUTES ● SERVES 4

140g/5oz soba noodles

300g/10oz fresh or frozen podded edamame (soy) beans

4 spring onions, shredded

300g bag beansprouts

1 cucumber, peeled, halved lengthways, deseeded with a teaspoon and sliced

1 tsp sesame oil

250g block firm tofu, patted dry and thickly sliced

1 tsp vegetable oil

handful of coriander leaves, to garnish

FOR THE DRESSING

3 tbsp mirin (rice wine)

2 tsp tamari sauce

2 tbsp orange juice

1 red chilli, deseeded, if you like, and finely chopped

1 Heat the dressing ingredients together in your smallest pan, simmer for just 30 seconds, then set aside.

2 Boil the noodles according to the pack instructions, adding the edamame beans for the final 2 minutes of the cooking time. Rinse under very cold water, drain thoroughly and tip into a large bowl with the spring onions, beansprouts, cucumber, sesame oil and warm dressing. Season if you like.

3 Brush the tofu with the vegetable oil, season and griddle or grill for 2–3 minutes each side – the tofu is very delicate so turn it carefully. Top the salad with the tofu, scatter with coriander leaves and serve.

PER SERVING 331 kcals, protein 21g, carbs 48g, fat 7g, sat fat 1g, fibre 5g, sugar 7g, salt 1.24g

Lemon & rosemary pork with chickpea salad

Ring the changes by making this dish with chicken breasts, or swapping the lemon for orange. Thyme makes a good substitute for the rosemary too.

TAKES 30 MINUTES, PLUS
MARINATING ● SERVES 4

1 tbsp olive oil
2 tsp finely chopped rosemary
4 garlic cloves, crushed
juice and zest of ½ lemon
4 boneless pork steaks, trimmed of fat
1 red onion, finely sliced
2 tbsp sherry vinegar
2 × 400g cans chickpeas, drained and rinsed
110g bag mixed salad leaves

1 Mix the olive oil, rosemary, garlic, lemon juice and zest in a large bowl. Add the pork, turn to coat and season well. If you have time, marinate in the fridge for 30 minutes.

2 Heat a large non-stick frying pan. Lift the pork out of the marinade, shaking off any excess and reserving the marinade. Cook the pork in the pan for 3–4 minutes each side or until cooked through. Leave to rest on a plate.

3 Pour the reserved marinade into the pan with the onion. Cook for 1 minute over a high heat before adding the vinegar, plus 3 tablespoons water. Bubble down for 1 minute, until the onion has softened and the dressing thickened slightly. Stir through the chickpeas, some seasoning and the resting juices from the pork. Put the salad leaves into a bowl, tip in the pan contents and gently toss. Serve immediately with the pork.

PER SERVING 396 kcals, protein 40g, carbs 23g, fat 17g, sat fat 3g, fibre 6g, sugar 3g, salt 0.90g

Hot tea-smoked trout with new potato & rocket salad

You can cook this home-smoked trout on a barbecue – simply wait for the coals to turn ashy grey, then follow the recipe, pop the tin on the grill and cook as below.

TAKES 35 MINUTES ● SERVES 4

500g/1lb 2oz baby new potatoes, larger ones halved
1 tsp Dijon mustard
2 tbsp olive oil
1 tbsp white wine vinegar
4 spring onions, sliced
10 tea bags (not herbal ones)
50g/2oz demerara sugar
50g/2oz long-grain rice
4 fresh trout, about 300–350g/10–12oz, gutted and heads removed
100g bag rocket leaves

1 Boil the potatoes in a pan of salted water for about 15 minutes. Drain well and steam dry for 5 minutes.

2 Mix together the mustard, oil and vinegar with some seasoning. Stir in the onions, then pour the dressing over the warm potatoes and allow to cool.

3 Split the tea bags and empty the leaves into a bowl with the sugar and rice. Line a deep roasting tin with foil, tip the smoking mix on top and cover with another piece of foil. Put the tin on the hob over a medium heat until it starts to smoke a little. Once you see smoke escaping, put the trout on top with some seasoning and cover with more foil, trapping the smoke inside. Lower the heat and leave for 20–22 minutes until the trout is cooked.

4 Stir the rocket into the potato salad. Divide among four plates and serve with the trout.

PER SERVING 393 kcals, protein 46g, carbs 21g, fat 14g, sat fat 3g, fibre none, sugar none, salt none

Chicken breast with avocado salad

The heat of the smoked paprika coating the chicken contrasts well with the coolness of the salad. A quick dinner for after work that can easily be doubled.

TAKES 20 MINUTES • SERVES 1

1 boneless skinless chicken breast
2 tsp olive oil
1 heaped tsp smoked paprika

FOR THE SALAD

½ small avocado, diced
1 medium tomato, chopped
½ small red onion, thinly sliced
1 tsp red wine vinegar
1 tbsp flat-leaf parsley, roughly
  chopped

1 Heat the grill to medium. Rub the chicken all over with 1 teaspoon of the olive oil and the paprika. Cook the chicken for 4–5 minutes on each side until lightly charred and cooked through.
2 Mix together the avocado, tomato and red onion. Whisk together the remaining oil, vinegar, parsley and some seasoning, and drizzle over the salad. Thickly slice the chicken and serve with the salad.

PER SERVING 344 kcals, protein 32g, carbs 9g, fat 20g, sat fat 4g, fibre 3g, sugar 5g, salt 0.23g

Big ham salad

You can use any leftover cold meat in this quick-to-put-together salad. Switch the herb to suit the meat so, for example, use chopped sage in the dressing with leftover pork.

TAKES 25 MINUTES ● SERVES 4
200g/7oz frozen peas, defrosted
250g/9oz ham, shredded or torn
2 Little Gem lettuces, leaves separated
bunch of spring onions, sliced
300g/10oz cooked new potatoes, sliced
small bunch of mint, roughly chopped
150g/5oz natural yogurt
1 tsp sugar

1 Cook the peas in boiling water for 1 minute. Drain and rinse under cold running water.
2 Toss the peas with the ham, lettuce, spring onions, potatoes and two-thirds of the mint. Mix the remaining mint with the yogurt and sugar. Drizzle the dressing over the salad and serve.

PER SERVING 217 kcals, protein 20g, carbs 23g, fat 5g, sat fat 2g, fibre 4g, sugar 7g, salt 1.80g

Warm chicken liver salad

An under-used ingredient, chicken livers are quick to cook, and this tasty and substantial salad is a good source of iron, folic acid and vitamin C.

TAKES 25 MINUTES • SERVES 4

140g/5oz fine green beans
200g/7oz chicken livers, trimmed
½ tbsp olive oil
½ tsp chopped fresh or dried rosemary
1 whole chicory or Baby Gem lettuce,
    separated into leaves
100g/4oz watercress
3 tbsp balsamic vinegar
crusty granary bread, to serve

1 Cook the green beans in a pan of boiling water for 3 minutes, drain and keep warm. Meanwhile, toss together the chicken livers, olive oil and rosemary. Heat a large non-stick pan and cook the chicken livers over a high heat for around 5–6 minutes until nicely browned and cooked through – they should still be a little pink in the centre.

2 Arrange the beans on serving plates with the lettuce leaves and watercress. Add the vinegar to the chicken livers in the pan, cook for a couple of seconds then spoon over the salad. Serve warm with crusty granary bread.

PER SERVING 83 kcals, protein 10g, carbs 4g, fat 3g, sat fat 1g, fibre 1g, sugar 3g, salt 0.13g

Hot-smoked salmon, double cress & potato salad platter

You can prepare all the elements of this salad in advance, apart from the avocado as it browns when cut. Then simply assemble the salad to serve.

TAKES 1 HOUR 10 MINUTES
- **SERVES 8**

400g/14oz small new potatoes
100g/4oz green beans
12 quail's eggs
2 packs hot-smoked salmon (about 350g/12oz in total)
2 avocados
2 × 100g bags watercress
1 head chicory, broken into leaves
5 spring onions, trimmed and sliced
1 pot mustard cress, trimmed

FOR THE DRESSING

1 heaped tbsp wholegrain mustard
1 heaped tsp clear honey
3 tbsp cider vinegar
8 tbsp olive oil

1 To make the dressing, whisk all the ingredients together in a bowl with some seasoning. Cook the potatoes in plenty of boiling water for 10 minutes until just tender. Drain, cool slightly, then slice.

2 Meanwhile, blanch the beans in boiling water for 4 minutes until cooked, drain, plunge into iced water, then drain again. Cook the quail's eggs for 3 minutes. Drain, put under cold water, then peel and halve. Flake the salmon into large chunks into a bowl. Just before serving, halve, peel and slice avocados.

3 This is a layered rather than a tossed salad, so start by scattering watercress and chicory over a platter. Scatter different handfuls at a time of all the other ingredients (but not the mustard cress). Drizzle over two-thirds of dressing, then strew over mustard cress to finish. Serve with the remaining dressing on the side.

PER SERVING 315 kcals, protein 15g, carbs 11g, fat 24g, sat fat 3g, fibre 3g, sugar 2g, salt 1.3g

Mustard griddled chicken, beetroot & orange salad

The combination of mustard, beetroot and oranges adds a fresh and zingy flavour to this tempting salad. Great for a quick supper or lunch with friends.

TAKES 30 MINUTES • SERVES 4

- 4 skinless chicken thigh fillets, sliced into thick strips
- 2 oranges
- 2 tbsp Dijon mustard
- 1 tbsp olive oil
- 140g bag spinach, rocket & watercress salad
- 4 vacuum-packed cooked beetroot, cut into wedges

1 Put the chicken between two sheets of baking parchment or cling film and bash with a rolling pin to flatten. Grate the zest from ½ orange and mix in a bowl with the mustard, 2 teaspoons of the oil and plenty of seasoning. Add the chicken and stir well.

2 Heat a griddle or frying pan and cook the chicken for 5–6 minutes on each side until cooked through. Put on a plate to rest while you assemble the salad.

3 Tip the salad leaves into a bowl. Peel and slice the oranges on a plate to catch any juices. Pour the orange juice over the leaves, add the orange slices with the remaining teaspoon of oil and toss together. Add the beetroot, then slice the chicken and add to the salad along with any resting juices. Divide everything among four plates and serve.

PER SERVING 205 kcals, protein 24g, carbs 14g, fat 6g, sat fat 1g, fibre 3g, sugar 13g, salt 1.09g

Harissa chicken with chickpea salad

The harissa gives a spicy aromatic flavour to the chicken, which can be cooked on a griddle or on the barbecue in summer. This tasty salad provides three of your 5-a-day.

TAKES 25 MINUTES ● **SERVES 2**

250g punnet cherry tomatoes, halved
½ small red onion, chopped
400g can chickpeas, drained and rinsed
small bunch of parsley, roughly
    chopped
juice of 1 lemon
2 boneless skinless chicken breasts,
    halved lengthways through the
    middle
1 tbsp harissa

TO SERVE

fat-free natural yogurt
wholemeal pitta bread

1 Mix the tomatoes, onion and chickpeas together. Stir through the parsley and lemon juice, and season.
2 Coat the chicken with the harissa. Heat a griddle or frying pan or barbecue. Cook the chicken for 3–4 minutes on each side until lightly charred and cooked through.
3 Divide the salad between two plates, top with the harissa chicken and serve with a dollop of yogurt and warmed pitta bread.

PER SERVING 313 kcals, protein 44g, carbs 25g, fat 5g, sat fat 1g, fibre 7g, sugar 6g, salt 1.06g

Zesty haddock with crushed potatoes & peas

Salmon fillets could replace the haddock here – just cook the fish for an extra few minutes. As well as being low in fat, this dish is a good source of vitamin C.

TAKES 35 MINUTES • SERVES 4

600g/1lb 5oz floury potatoes, unpeeled, cut into chunks
140g/5oz frozen peas
2½ tbsp extra virgin olive oil
juice and zest of ½ lemon
1 tbsp capers, roughly chopped
2 tbsp snipped chives
4 haddock or other chunky white fish fillets, about 120g/4½oz each
2 tbsp plain flour
steamed broccoli, to serve

1 Cover the potatoes in cold water in a pan, bring to the boil, then lower to a simmer. Cook for 10 minutes until tender, adding the peas for the final minute of cooking. Drain and roughly crush together, adding plenty of seasoning and 1 tablespoon of the oil. Keep warm.

2 Meanwhile, for the dressing, mix 1 tablespoon of the oil, the lemon juice and zest, capers and chives with some seasoning. Set aside.

3 Dust the fish in the flour, tapping off any excess, and season. Heat the remaining oil in a non-stick frying pan. Fry the fish for 2–3 minutes on each side until cooked, then add the dressing and warm through. Serve with the potato and pea crush and steamed broccoli.

PER SERVING 305 kcals, protein 28g, carbs 31g, fat 8g, sat fat 1g, fibre 4g, sugar 2g, salt 0.71g

Somerset stew

This recipe packs in three of your 5-a-day and is also a good source of vitamins, making it a healthy family supper. Use your own favourite canned beans.

TAKES 50 MINUTES • SERVES 4

1 tbsp oil
1 onion, finely chopped
1 garlic clove, finely chopped
1 large carrot, finely chopped
1 leek, chopped
1 tbsp tomato purée
400g can chopped tomatoes
200g can butter beans, drained and
    rinsed
400g can flageolet beans, drained
    and rinsed
200ml/7fl oz dry cider
250ml/9fl oz vegetable stock
few thyme sprigs, leaves only
mashed potato and chopped parsley,
    to serve

1 Heat the oil in a large pan and fry the onion, garlic, carrot and leek until soft but not coloured.

2 Add all the remaining ingredients and simmer for 15–20 minutes until the stew has thickened and the vegetables are tender. Serve with some mashed potato with a handful of chopped parsley stirred through it.

PER SERVING 169 kcals, protein 9g, carbs 24g, fat 4g, sat fat none, fibre 7g, sugar 10g, salt 0.99g

Classic chunky fish cakes

If you fancy a bit of spice, add 1–2 tablespoons of your favourite curry paste to the mixture and swap the herbs for a large handful of chopped coriander.

TAKES 1 HOUR 20 MINUTES
- **MAKES 12**

1kg/2lb 4oz potatoes, peeled and chopped

1kg/2lb 4oz mixed salmon and coley fillets

zest and juice of 1 lemon

bunch each of dill, chives, parsley and spring onions, chopped

4 tbsp tartare sauce, plus extra to serve, if you like

3 eggs, beaten

100g/4oz plain flour

250g/9oz breadcrumbs

2 tbsp olive oil

1 Cover the potatoes with cold, salted water and bring to the boil. Turn down and simmer for 10–12 minutes until tender. Drain and steam dry for a few minutes, then mash and set aside to cool.

2 Meanwhile, poach the fish in water with the lemon juice for 5 minutes (depending on the thickness of the fish) until just cooked through. Remove, discard the skin and flake into large chunks.

3 Combine the zest, herbs, onions, tartare sauce and some seasoning in a large bowl with the fish and potatoes. Divide into 12 and shape into cakes.

4 Put the eggs, flour and breadcrumbs on three separate plates. Dip each fish cake first in the flour, pat off any excess, then dip in the egg. Finally, coat in breadcrumbs and transfer to a clean plate. Repeat with the remaining fish cakes.

5 Heat grill to medium. Brush the fish cakes with oil and grill for 4–5 minutes on each side until golden and hot throughout.

PER CAKE 330 kcals, protein 23g, carbs 38g, fat 10g, sat fat 2g, fibre 2g, sugar 2g, salt 0.71g

Chicken & chorizo jambalaya

A good family one-pot that's quick to prepare and can then be left to simmer away on the hob. Leftover Cajun spice is great stirred into roasted vegetables before cooking.

TAKES 55 MINUTES • SERVES 4

1 tbsp olive oil
2 boneless skinless chicken breasts, chopped
1 onion, diced
1 red pepper, deseeded and thinly sliced
2 garlic cloves, crushed
75g/2½oz chorizo, sliced
1 tbsp Cajun seasoning
250g/9oz long grain rice
400g can plum tomatoes
350ml/12fl oz chicken stock

1 Heat the oil in a large frying pan with a lid and brown the chicken for 5–8 minutes until golden. Remove and set aside. Tip in the onion and cook for 3–4 minutes until soft. Then add the pepper, garlic, chorizo and Cajun seasoning, and cook for 5 minutes more.
2 Stir the chicken back into the pan with the rice, and add the tomatoes and stock. Cover and simmer for around 20–25 minutes until the rice is tender.

PER SERVING 445 kcals, protein 30g, carbs 64g, fat 10g, sat fat 3g, fibre 2g, sugar 7g, salt 1.2g

Smoky beef stew

Make this for a family supper and then turn the leftovers into packed lunches to take to work. It's great wrapped topped with crumbled feta and served with pitta.

TAKES 3 HOURS 10 MINUTES

● **SERVES 6–8**

1kg/2lb 4oz stewing beef, cut into large chunks
2 onions, chopped
2 × 400g cans chopped tomatoes
2 tsp each sweet paprika, ground cumin and mild chilli powder
2 tbsp red or white vinegar
2 tbsp caster sugar
400g can butter beans, drained and rinsed

1 Heat oven to 160C/140C fan/gas 3. Mix the beef, onions, tomatoes, spices, vinegar and sugar in a casserole dish. Cover and cook for 2½ hours.

2 Stir in the beans and cook for another 30 minutes (with the lid off if you find that the casserole is a little wet or lid on if it is a good consistency), until the beef is tender. Serve half as a supper with mash and broccoli.

3 Cool the remainder, then freeze in portions in small food bags or plastic containers. Defrost in the microwave or overnight in fridge, then heat in the morning and transfer to a flask, or heat in the microwave at lunchtime.

PER SERVING (6) 341 kcals, protein 42g, carbs 18g, fat 12g, sat fat 5g, fibre 4g, sugar 11g, salt 0.92g

Artichoke, red onion & rosemary risotto

To ring the changes in this creamy risotto, leave out the rosemary and stir in 85g/3oz diced lean ham with a handful of basil leaves. Drizzle with balsamic vinegar to serve.

TAKES 50 MINUTES • SERVES 4

1 tbsp olive oil

2 red onions, sliced into thin wedges

2 red peppers, deseeded and cut into chunks

2 tbsp rosemary leaves

140g/5oz arborio risotto rice

150ml/¼ pint white wine

850ml/1½ pints low-salt vegetable stock

400g can artichoke hearts in water, drained and halved

2 tbsp grated Parmesan

2 tbsp toasted pine nuts

1 Heat the oil in a large frying pan or wok. Cook the onions gently for 6–7 minutes until softened and browning. Add the peppers and rosemary, and cook for a further 5 minutes. Add the rice and stir well.

2 Pour in the wine and one-third of the stock. Bring the risotto to the boil then reduce the heat and simmer gently, stirring occasionally, until almost all the liquid is absorbed.

3 Stir in another one-third of the stock and simmer again, until it's all absorbed. Add the remaining stock with the artichokes and simmer again until the rice is tender.

4 Season and stir in the Parmesan and half the pine nuts. Scatter over the remaining pine nuts to serve.

PER SERVING 299 kcals, protein 9g, carbs 44g, fat 10g, sat fat 2g, fibre 4g, sugar 9g, salt 0.65g

Spicy Cajun chicken quinoa

Quinoa is a healthy alternative to rice or pasta as it provides good levels of protein and is also an excellent source of calcium, iron, fibre and B vitamins. It's gluten-free, too.

TAKES 35 MINUTES ● SERVES 4

4 boneless skinless chicken breasts, cut into bite-size pieces
1 tbsp Cajun spice mix
100g/4oz quinoa
600ml/1 pint hot chicken stock
100g/4oz dried apricots, sliced
½ × 250g pouch ready-to-use Puy lentils
1 tbsp olive oil
2 red onions, cut into thin wedges
1 bunch spring onions, chopped
small bunch of coriander, chopped

1 Heat oven to 200C/180C fan/gas 6. Toss the chicken with the Cajun spice and arrange in a single layer in a roasting tin. Bake for 20 minutes until the chicken is cooked. Set aside.

2 Meanwhile, cook the quinoa in the chicken stock for 15 minutes until tender, adding the apricots and lentils for the final 5 minutes. Drain and put in a large bowl with the chicken and toss together.

3 While the quinoa is cooking, heat the oil in a large frying pan and soften the onions for 10–15 minutes. Toss the onions into the quinoa–chicken mix with the coriander and some seasoning, then mix well and serve.

PER SERVING 386 kcals, protein 47g, carbs 35g, fat 7g, sat fat 1g, fibre 5g, sugar 15g, salt 1g

Ricotta, tomato & spinach frittata

Served with a leafy salad and chunks of crusty bread, this colourful pizza-look supper gets the thumbs-up from the younger members of the family.

TAKES 45 MINUTES • SERVES 4

1 tbsp olive oil
1 large onion, finely sliced
300g/10oz cherry tomatoes
100g/4oz spinach leaves
small handful of basil leaves
100g/4oz ricotta
6 eggs, beaten
salad, to serve

1 Heat oven to 200C/180C fan/gas 6. Heat the oil in a large non-stick frying pan and cook the onion for 5–6 minutes until softened and lightly golden. Add the cherry tomatoes to the pan and toss for 1 minute to soften.

2 Remove from the heat, add the spinach leaves and basil, and toss together to wilt a little. Transfer all the ingredients to a greased 30 x 20cm rectangular baking tin. Take small scoops of the ricotta and dot them evenly over the vegetables.

3 Season the eggs and beat well, then pour over the vegetables and cheese. Cook in the oven for 20–25 minutes until pale golden and set. Serve with salad.

PER SERVING 236 kcals, protein 16g, carbs 7g, fat 16g, sat fat 5g, fibre 2g, sugar 6g, salt 0.5g

Mediterranean vegetables with lamb

The lamb is beautifully tender and the vegetables taste amazing, especially the shallots, which give this supper a sweet touch. The veg provide three of your 5-a-day.

TAKES 45 MINUTES • SERVES 4

1 tbsp olive oil
250g/9oz lean lamb fillet, trimmed of
    any fat and thinly sliced
140g/5oz shallots, halved
2 large courgettes, cut into chunks
½ tsp each ground cumin, paprika and
    ground coriander
1 red, 1 orange and 1 green pepper,
    deseeded and cut into chunks
1 garlic clove, sliced
150ml/¼ pint vegetable stock
250g/9oz cherry tomatoes
handful of coriander leaves, roughly
    chopped

1 Heat the oil in a large heavy-based frying pan. Cook the lamb and shallots over a high heat for 2–3 minutes until golden. Add the courgette chunks and stir-fry for 3–4 minutes until beginning to soften.

2 Add the spices and toss well, then add the peppers and garlic. Reduce the heat and cook over a moderate heat for 4–5 minutes until they start to soften.

3 Pour in the stock and stir to coat. Add the tomatoes, season, then cover with a lid and simmer for 15 minutes, stirring occasionally until the veg are tender. Stir through the coriander to serve.

PER SERVING 192 kcals, protein 17g, carbs 11g, fat 9g, sat fat 3g, fibre 4g, sugar 10g, salt 0.25g

Low-fat moussaka

Packed with veg, this recipe contains five of your 5-a-day and is a good source of iron and vitamin C. Plus it won't break the weekly budget either.

TAKES 55 MINUTES ● SERVES 4

200g/7oz frozen sliced peppers
3 garlic cloves, crushed
200g/7oz extra-lean minced beef
100g/4oz red split lentils
2 tsp dried oregano, plus extra for
    sprinkling
500ml carton passata
1 aubergine, sliced into 0.5cm/¼in
    rounds
4 tomatoes, sliced into 1cm/½in rounds
2 tsp olive oil
25g/1oz Parmesan, finely grated
170g pot 0% fat Greek yogurt
freshly grated nutmeg

1 Cook the peppers gently in a non-stick pan for about 5 minutes. Add the garlic and cook for 1 minute, then add the beef, breaking it up with a fork, and cook until brown. Tip in the lentils, half the oregano, the passata and a splash of water. Simmer for 15–20 minutes, adding more water if you need to.

2 Meanwhile, heat grill to medium. Arrange the aubergine and tomato slices on a non-stick baking sheet and brush with the oil. Sprinkle with the remaining oregano and some seasoning. Grill for 1–2 minutes each side until charred – you may need to do this in batches.

3 Mix half the Parmesan with the yogurt and some seasoning. Divide the beef mixture among four small ovenproof dishes and top with the aubergine and tomato. Spoon over the yogurt topping and sprinkle with extra oregano, the remaining Parmesan and the nutmeg. Grill for 3–4 minutes until bubbling.

PER SERVING 289 kcals, protein 26g, carbs 31g, fat 8g, sat fat 3g, fibre 5g, sugar 12g, salt 1.00g

Baked fennel pork with lemony potatoes & onions

As the potatoes are cooked in this one-pot with the pork, all you need to round off the meal is a little broccoli and some chunks of crusty bread, if you like.

TAKES 1 HOUR 5 MINUTES • SERVES 4

2 tbsp fennel seeds
1 tbsp olive oil
4 pork loin steaks, trimmed of fat
1 large onion, sliced
2 garlic cloves, thinly sliced
750g/1lb 10oz baby new potatoes,
    halved lengthways
2 fennel bulbs, thinly sliced, green
    fronds reserved
juice of 2 lemons
350g/12oz broccoli, broken into florets

1 Crush the fennel seeds lightly in a pestle and mortar. Mix with half the oil and a little seasoning. Rub into the pork and set aside.

2 Heat oven to 200C/180C fan/gas 6. Heat the remaining oil in a shallow ovenproof dish. Soften the onion and garlic for about 5 minutes, then tip in the potatoes and brown for a few minutes. Add the fennel, lemon juice and about 100ml/3½fl oz water. Season, cover with the lid and cook in the oven for 35 minutes.

3 Remove the lid, stir the potatoes and put the meat on top. Return to the oven, uncovered, and cook for another 10 minutes or until the pork is cooked to your liking. Meanwhile, cook the broccoli.

4 Scatter the reserved fennel fronds over the pork and serve with the broccoli.

PER SERVING 407 kcals, protein 40g, carbs 40g, fat 11g, sat fat 3g, fibre 7g, sugar 8g, salt 0.33g

Spicy baby aubergine stew with coriander & mint

You'll find baby aubergines in Asian stores and some supermarkets. Aubergines are packed with heart-friendly nutrients, and this dish provides five of your 5-a-day.

TAKES 55 MINUTES • SERVES 4

2 tbsp olive oil

2 red onions, sliced

4 garlic cloves, smashed

2 red chillies, deseeded and sliced, or 2–3 dried red chillies, left whole

2 tsp coriander seeds, toasted and crushed

2 tsp cumin seeds, toasted and crushed

16 baby aubergines, left whole with stalk intact

2 × 400g cans chopped tomatoes

2 tsp sugar

bunch of mint leaves, roughly chopped

bunch of coriander, roughly chopped

couscous and natural yogurt, to serve

1 Heat the oil in a heavy-based pan, add the onions and garlic, and cook until they begin to colour. Add the chillies and crushed coriander and cumin seeds. When the seeds give off a nutty aroma, toss in the whole aubergines, coating them in the onion and spices.

2 Tip in the tomatoes and sugar, cover and gently cook for 40 minutes, until the aubergines are tender.

3 Season the sauce and toss in half the mint and coriander. Cover and simmer for 2 minutes. Sprinkle over the remaining herbs and serve with couscous and natural yogurt.

PER SERVING 148 kcals, protein 5g, carbs 16g, fat 7g, sat fat 1g, fibre 6g, sugar 13g, salt 0.31g

Beef schnitzel

Children love this dish and will enjoy helping with the prep by dipping the minute steaks in flour, egg and breadcrumbs for the crispy coating.

TAKES 35 MINUTES ● **SERVES 5**

5 thin-cut minute steaks
50g/2oz plain flour
2 tsp paprika
2 eggs, lightly beaten
250g/9oz dried breadcrumbs
5 tsp butter
5 tsp olive oil
lemon wedges, to garnish
salad and coleslaw, to serve (optional)

1 Stretch a piece of cling film over a chopping board, lay the steaks on top of it, then put another piece of cling film on top. Use a rolling pin to bash the steaks until they are really flat and thin.
2 Mix the flour and paprika with some salt and pepper on a plate. Put the egg and breadcrumbs on two more plates, then dip the steaks into the flour first, then the egg, then the breadcrumbs.
3 Heat 1 teaspoon of the butter and 1 teaspoon of the oil in a large frying pan, then cook one of the schnitzels for about 1 minute on each side until the breadcrumbs are golden and crispy. Keep warm while you cook the other schnitzels. Serve with lemon wedges, salad and coleslaw, if you like.

PER SERVING 468 kcals, protein 43g, carbs 46g, fat 14g, sat fat 4g, fibre 2g, sugar 3g, salt 0.82g

Baked courgettes stuffed with spiced lamb & tomato sauce

Serve this hearty bake warm rather than hot, with chunks of crusty bread to mop up the spicy sauce. This recipe will also work with marrow.

TAKES 1¼ HOURS ● SERVES 4

4 large courgettes, halved lengthways
1 tbsp olive oil
small handful of coriander leaves,
   to sprinkle

FOR THE TOMATO SAUCE

1 tbsp olive oil
4 garlic cloves, crushed
1 tsp each ground cayenne pepper,
   cinnamon, coriander and cumin
2 × 400g cans chopped tomatoes
2 tsp sugar

FOR THE STUFFING

500g/1lb 2oz lean minced lamb
2 tsp each ground cumin, coriander
   and cinnamon
1 tsp cayenne pepper

1 Heat oven to 220C/200C fan/gas 7. First make the tomato sauce. Heat the oil in a medium pan and fry the garlic for 2–3 minutes until soft. Add the spices and fry for 1 minute more. Pour in the tomatoes, half a can of water and the sugar and simmer for 20 minutes, until thickened. Season.

2 Meanwhile, scoop out and discard some of the flesh of the courgettes and lay them in one large or two small roasting tins, drizzle with the oil and bake for 15 minutes until golden and softened slightly.

3 For the stuffing, lightly mix the lamb with the spices and some salt with your hands until just combined. When the courgettes are ready, pile the lamb into the cavities and drizzle over the sauce. Bake for 15–20 minutes until the sauce is bubbling. Sprinkle with the coriander and serve.

PER SERVING 200 kcals, protein 16g, carbs 8g, fat 12g, sat fat 4g, fibre 2g, sugar 5g, salt 0.3g

Pork Milanese with spaghetti

The tomatoey sauce-coated pasta topped with the crispy-crumb pork fillets combine for a sure-fire winning supper with all the family.

TAKES 45 MINUTES • SERVES 4

1 tbsp olive oil
1 garlic clove, crushed
2 × 400g cans chopped tomatoes
2 tsp balsamic vinegar
420g pack pork fillet, sliced into
    8 medallions
2 tbsp plain flour
1 egg, beaten
100g/4oz fresh breadcrumbs
300g/10oz spaghetti
small bunch of basil, chopped

1 Heat the oil in a pan, then fry the garlic for a few seconds. Add the chopped tomatoes and balsamic vinegar, and bubble for about 15–20 minutes until the sauce is thick.

2 Meanwhile, lay the pork medallions between two layers of cling film and bash with a rolling pin until they are about 1cm/½in thick. Mix the flour with some seasoning on one plate, put the egg on another and the breadcrumbs on a third.Dip the pork in the flour, then the egg, then the breadcrumbs. Heat the grill to high, then cook the pork for 3 minutes on each side, until golden and cooked through. Keep warm.

3 Cook the pasta according to the pack instructions. Drain the spaghetti and stir through the tomato sauce with the chopped basil. Divide the pasta and sauce among four plates, lay the crispy pork on top and eat immediately.

PER SERVING 597 kcals, protein 40g, carbs 85g, fat 13g, sat fat 4g, fibre 5g, sugar 9g, salt 1.00g

Indian-spiced shepherd's pie

Give a much loved favourite a new flavour with this spicy version and top with diced turmeric potatoes. You'll love this as much as the original.

TAKES 1 HOUR 5 MINUTES • SERVES 6

500g pack lean minced lamb
1 onion, chopped
2 carrots, diced
2 tbsp garam masala
200ml/7fl oz hot stock (lamb, beef or chicken)
200g/7oz frozen peas
800g/1lb 12oz potatoes, diced
1 tsp ground turmeric
small bunch of coriander, roughly chopped
juice of ½ lemon, plus wedges to garnish

1 In a non-stick frying pan, cook the lamb, onion and carrots, stirring often, until the lamb is browned and the vegetables are starting to soften, about 8 minutes. Add the garam masala and some seasoning, and cook for a further 2 minutes. Pour in the stock, bring to the boil, tip in the peas and cook for a further 2 minutes until most of the liquid has evaporated.

2 Meanwhile, cook the potatoes in a large pan of salted boiling water until just tender, about 8 minutes. Drain well, return to the pan and gently stir in the turmeric and coriander – try not to break up the potatoes too much.

3 Heat oven to 200C/180C fan/gas 6. Transfer the mince to a baking dish and top with the turmeric potatoes. Squeeze over the lemon juice, then bake for 30–35 minutes until the potatoes are golden. Serve immediately with extra lemon wedges on the side.

PER SERVING 317 kcals, protein 22g, carbs 32g, fat 12g, sat fat 5g, fibre 4g, sugar 5g, salt 0.44g

Grilled mackerel with soy, lime & ginger

Mackerel are always a great buy and are a good source of omega-3. The ginger and lime marinade makes an ideal foil for the oiliness of the fish.

TAKES 25 MINUTES, PLUS MARINATING • SERVES 2

300g/10oz mackerel fillets
100g/4oz jasmine rice
4 spring onions, sliced
1 red pepper, deseeded and diced

FOR THE MARINADE

1 tbsp low-sodium soy sauce
juice of 1 lime
small piece of ginger, grated
1 garlic clove, crushed
2 tbsp clear honey

1 To make the marinade, mix all the ingredients together and pour over the mackerel. Cover and chill for 30 minutes.

2 Heat grill and put the mackerel, skin-side up, on a baking sheet lined with foil. Grill for 5 minutes, then turn and baste with the reserved marinade. Grill for 5 minutes more.

3 Cook the rice according to the pack instructions, then drain and toss with the spring onions and red pepper. Serve the rice with the mackerel.

PER SERVING 587 kcals, protein 33g, carbs 61g, fat 25g, sat fat 5g, fibre 1g, sugar 17g, salt 1.10g

Ham hock & cabbage hash

A really filling, really tasty low-fat supper that's a moneywise choice too. Serve with baked beans, brown sauce or tomato ketchup and some crusty bread.

TAKES 50 MINUTES ● SERVES 5

1kg/2lb 4oz potatoes, unpeeled and
    cut into cubes
25g/1oz butter
½ Savoy cabbage, shredded
1 onion, thinly sliced
100ml/3½fl oz low-sodium vegetable
    stock
175g/6oz ham hock, shredded
baked beans, to serve (optional)

1 Cook the potatoes in a large pan of salted water until tender, drain, then allow to steam dry for about 3 minutes.
2 Meanwhile, melt half the butter in a large non-stick frying pan, then throw in the cabbage and onion, and fry for 2 minutes. Add the stock and cook for 5 minutes more until the veg is starting to soften. Stir in the ham and potatoes, and push down in the pan to flatten slightly. Cook for 8 minutes until the base is golden and crisp.
3 Heat the grill. Dot the remaining butter on top of the hash, then flash under the grill until golden and crisp. Serve with baked beans, brown sauce or ketchup, if you like.

PER SERVING 263 kcals, protein 14g, carbs 40g, fat 7g, sat fat 3g, fibre 5g, sugar 5g, salt 0.88g

Roast pork with apples & mustard

Apples and sage are classic partners for pork and they make this a popular family dish, as children love the fruity flavour. Serve with mash and steamed broccoli.

TAKES 50 MINUTES • SERVES 4

1 tbsp olive oil

3 eating apples

500g/1lb 2oz pork fillet, sliced into medallions

200ml/7fl oz reduced-salt chicken stock

1 tbsp wholegrain mustard

1 tbsp chopped sage leaves

2 tbsp half-fat crème fraîche

1 Heat half the oil in a large frying pan. Core and cut the apples into wedges, then cook in the oil for about 10 minutes until caramelised and softened. Remove from the pan and set aside.

2 Heat the remaining oil in the pan. Fry the pork on each side for 2 minutes. Add the stock and mustard to the pan, then bubble for 5 minutes or until the pork is cooked through. Return the apples to the pan with the sage and cook for 1 minute more. Remove from the heat and stir in the crème fraîche and some seasoning before serving.

PER SERVING 246 kcals, protein 28g, carbs 12g, fat 10g, sat fat 3g, fibre 2g, sugar 11g, salt 0.39g

Chicken & vegetable stew with wholemeal couscous

Using wholegrains, such as wholemeal couscous, makes sense nutritionally as they are rich in vitamins, minerals and fibre.

TAKES 40 MINUTES ● **SERVES 2**

1 tbsp olive oil
2 boneless skinless chicken breasts, cut into chunks
1 small onion, sliced
1 garlic clove, crushed
pinch each of paprika and saffron
50g/2oz baby sweetcorn, halved
50g/2oz asparagus tips
50g/2oz peas
50g/2oz cherry tomatoes, halved
150ml/¼ pint chicken stock
140g/5oz wholemeal couscous

1 Heat the oil in a pan, add the chicken and cook for 5–6 minutes, then remove with a slotted spoon. Set aside. Add the onion to the pan and cook for around 2–3 minutes before adding the garlic, paprika, saffron, sweetcorn, asparagus, peas and tomatoes. Cook for a further 2–3 minutes. Return the chicken to the pan, pour in the stock, then cover and simmer for 15 minutes.

2 Meanwhile, cook the couscous according to the pack instructions. To serve, fluff the couscous with a fork and divide between two bowls before spooning over the stew.

PER SERVING 347 kcals, protein 32g, carbs 46g, fat 5g, sat fat 1g, fibre 3g, sugar 5g, salt 0.2g

Tandoori lamb skewers with crunchy slaw & raita

This fantastic – and colourful – recipe contains three of your 5-a-day fruit-and-veg portions, so it makes a great healthy supper. It's easily doubled or trebled.

TAKES 20 MINUTES • SERVES 2

4 tbsp 0% fat Greek yogurt

1 tbsp tandoori paste

175g/6oz leg of lamb steak, all visible fat removed, cubed

small bunch of coriander, chopped

2 wholemeal chapatis, to serve

FOR THE SLAW

1 carrot, peeled and sliced into strips with a peeler

¼ white cabbage, shredded

1 red onion, sliced

juice of 1 lime

2 tsp olive oil

1 tsp mustard seeds

1 In a medium bowl, combine the tandoori paste with 2 tablespoons of the yogurt. Add the lamb, mixing to coat all the pieces.

2 Make the raita by mixing the remaining yogurt with 1 tablespoon of the chopped coriander and some seasoning, then set aside. For the slaw, mix together all of the vegetables and the remaining coriander in a large bowl, then stir in the lime juice, oil and mustard seeds.

3 Heat the grill to high. Divide the lamb among four skewers, grill for 3–4 minutes on each side, until lightly charred and cooked through. Serve with the slaw, raita and warmed chapatis.

PER SERVING 441 kcals, protein 30g, carbs 41g, fat 18g, sat fat 5g, fibre 8g, sugar 16g, salt 1.14g

Spicy mini meatloaves

These can be frozen uncooked. Cook from frozen at 180C/160C fan/gas 4, covered with foil, for 30 minutes. Remove foil and cook at 220C/200C fan/gas 7 for 25 minutes.

TAKES 45 MINUTES • SERVES 8

1kg/2lb 4oz lean minced beef
100g/4oz white breadcrumbs
3 spring onions, trimmed and finely chopped
2 garlic cloves, crushed
2 eggs, beaten
2 tsp ground cumin
½ tsp Tabasco (optional)
handful of coriander leaves, finely chopped
12 cherry tomatoes, halved
6–8 tbsp chilli sauce (optional)
vegetable oil, for greasing
roasted sweet potatoes and green salad, to serve

1 Mix together the beef, breadcrumbs, spring onions, garlic, eggs, cumin, Tabasco, if using, coriander and some seasoning until combined. Be careful not to over-mix or the meatloaves will be tough.

2 Heat oven to 200C/180C fan/gas 6. Divide the mixture into eight. Use your hands to shape each one into a small oval, like a mini meatloaf. Arrange 3 cherry tomatoes on top of each, then drizzle over the chilli sauce, if using.

3 Put the meatloaves on a lightly greased, shallow baking tin and bake for 25–30 minutes until the meat is cooked through. Serve with roasted sweet potatoes and a green salad.

PER SERVING 241 kcals, protein 31g, carbs 10g, fat 8g, sat fat 2g, fibre 1g, sugar 1g, salt 0.50g

Baked butternut squash, chickpeas & green chilli

Pomegranate seeds add a lovely fresh texture. If you can't find molasses, a few tablespoons of lime and a teaspoon of brown sugar work well drizzled over the top.

TAKES 1¼ HOURS ● **SERVES 4–6**

1kg/2lb 4oz butternut squash, deseeded and cut into chunks
3 tbsp olive oil
1 onion, finely chopped
3 garlic cloves, finely chopped
medium piece ginger, grated
1 green chilli, finely diced
2 tsp smoked paprika
400g can chopped tomatoes
2 tbsp pomegranate molasses
400g can chickpeas, drained and rinsed
chopped parsley, pomegranate seeds and mint leaves, to garnish
Greek yogurt and couscous, to serve

1 Heat oven to 180C/160C fan/gas 4. Put the squash on a baking sheet, drizzle with 2 tablespoons of the oil, season, toss to coat and roast for 25 minutes until tender. Leave the oven on.

2 Transfer half of the squash to a casserole dish; set aside the remainder. Put a medium-size frying pan on the heat and add the remaining oil, then the onion, garlic, ginger, chilli and paprika. Cook everything for 5–8 minutes. Pour in the tomatoes, pomegranate and chickpeas then mix well, simmer for 1 minute and turn off the heat.

3 Pour half the sauce over the squash in the casserole. Arrange the remaining squash pieces on top then finish with rest of the sauce. Cover, transfer to the oven and bake for 25 minutes.

4 Remove from the oven and serve scattered with parsley, pomegranate seeds and mint, with the yogurt on the side. Serve with couscous.

PER SERVING (4) 291 kcals, protein 9g, carbs 42g, fat 11g, sat fat 1g, fibre 8g, sugar 20g, salt 0.50g

Pan-fried salmon with watercress & polenta croûtons

Salmon and watercress are a natural partnership. This main course looks top-notch and tastes fabulous but is easy to cook. It is a good source of omega-3s too.

TAKES 30 MINUTES ● SERVES 6

250g/9oz cooked polenta, either
    bought ready-made or made from
    the grain (follow pack instructions
    and allow it to cool and set on a tray)
50g/2oz plain flour
3 tbsp olive oil, plus extra to dress
6 boneless skinless salmon fillets,
    about 140g/5oz each
200g/7oz watercress, washed and
    thick stalks removed
squeeze of lemon juice
2 tbsp capers in brine, drained

1 Cut the polenta into approximately 1.5cm/¾in cubes, toss in the flour and fry in a little oil until slightly coloured. Keep warm.

2 Heat oven to 190C/170C fan/gas 5. Heat the remaining oil in a non-stick pan and fry the salmon portions for 1 minute on each side until lightly golden, then transfer to a non-stick baking sheet and cook in the oven for 8–10 minutes. Test the fish to see if it is cooked by pushing a cocktail stick into the top of it. If the fish offers resistance, it is not fully cooked and will need further cooking. When cooked, remove from the oven and set aside.

3 Dress the watercress with a little olive oil and a few drops of lemon juice. Scatter the polenta croûtons and the capers over each salmon fillet and serve with the watercress.

PER SERVING 367 kcals, protein 31g, carbs 13g, fat 22g, sat fat 4g, fibre 2g, sugar 1g, salt 0.66g

Duck, apricot & pine nut pastilla

This impressive dinner-party pie is worth every bit of effort. North African brik pastry is traditionally used, but it can be hard to find – if you can't get it, use filo in its place.

TAKES 1 HOUR 50 MINUTES
- **SERVES 6**

6 confit duck legs (buy ready-prepared)
2 onions, chopped
1 tbsp olive oil, plus extra for brushing
140g/5oz dried apricots, quartered
1 tbsp ground cinnamon, plus a pinch extra for dusting
½ tbsp ground coriander
½ tbsp ground cumin
1 tsp fennel seeds
tiny pinch of saffron
400ml/14fl oz chicken stock
zest of 2 lemons, plus a good squeeze juice
50g/2oz toasted pine nuts, plus a few extra to garnish
4 large sheets brik or filo pastry

1 Shred the duck meat from the bones and set aside. Discard the skin and bones.

2 Gently fry the onions in the oil until softened and golden. Stir in the apricots and spices, and cook for 5 minutes, then pour in the stock. Stir in the duck and cook gently until moist, but not too liquid. Stir in the lemon zest, a squeeze of juice and the pine nuts. Season well.

3 Put a baking sheet in the oven and heat to 220C/200C fan/gas 7. Brush a 22–23cm-round springform or loose-bottomed baking tin with a little oil. Push two pastry sheets into the tin, lining the base and leaving extra up the sides. Spoon in the duck mixture and pat down evenly. Sit the other two sheets on top, scrunching the edges of the pastry around the sides. Brush the top with a little more oil and bake on the baking sheet for 20–30 minutes until crisp and golden brown. To serve, scatter with pine nuts and dust with cinnamon.

PER SERVING 359 kcals, protein 23g, carbs 26g, fat 19g, sat fat 3g, fibre 3g, sugar 13g, salt 0.79g

Rich braised beef with melting onions

Beef shin cooks to a melting texture far better than braising steak, which can become dry. You can make this dish up to 3 days ahead and store it in the fridge.

TAKES 2 HOURS 35 MINUTES
- **SERVES 4**

4 thick generous slices beef shin, about 700g/1lb 9oz total
plain flour, for dusting
2 tbsp sunflower oil
3 medium onions, halved and thinly sliced
2 tsp caster sugar
6 garlic cloves, sliced
700ml/1¼ pints beef stock (made with 2 cubes)
3 tbsp Worcestershire sauce
4 large flat mushrooms, thickly sliced
chopped parsley, to garnish

1 Dust the beef in the flour, then set aside. Heat the oil in a large pan. Add the onions and fry for 5 minutes. Add the sugar and cook for 5–10 minutes, stirring frequently, until the onions are caramelised. Stir in the garlic for the final few minutes.

2 Pour in the stock and stir in the Worcestershire sauce. Add the beef and mushrooms, then season, adding plenty of black pepper. Cover and cook gently for 2 hours until the meat is tender. Serve scattered with parsley.

PER SERVING 364 kcals, protein 44g, carbs 11g, fat 16g, sat fat 5g, fibre 2g, sugar 8g, salt 1.03g

Chicken biryani bake

This is a great dish for entertaining friends because it can be made ahead and frozen. Defrost and cook as below, just adding an extra 10–15 minutes to the cooking time.

TAKES 1 HOUR 25 MINUTES

● **SERVES 8**

2 tbsp olive oil

4 boneless skinless chicken breasts, chopped into chunks

4 boneless skinless chicken thighs, chopped into chunks

2 onions, sliced

4 tbsp korma or tikka masala curry paste

300g/10oz cauliflower, chopped into small florets

700ml/1¼ pints chicken stock

400g can chopped tomatoes

400g can chickpeas, drained and rinsed

200g/7oz natural yogurt

300g/10oz spinach leaves

400g/14oz basmati rice, cooked according to the pack instructions

5 tbsp flaked almonds

1 Heat 1 tablespoon of the oil in a large, deep frying pan. Season the chicken and fry until browned, then set aside. Fry the onions in the rest of the oil for 10–12 minutes until starting to caramelise.

2 Add the curry paste and cauliflower, stirring to coat, then return the chicken to the pan. Pour in the stock, tomatoes and chickpeas, and simmer for around 30 minutes until the cauliflower is tender. There should be enough liquid to cover everything, but add a splash more stock if you need to. Remove from the heat and stir in the yogurt.

3 Heat oven to 220C/200C fan/gas 7. Assemble the bake in a large, deep ovenproof dish. Start with a third of the spinach, season, then top with a third of the curry. Finish with a third of the rice then repeat the layers twice more. Scatter the almonds on top and cook for 20–25 minutes until the topping is crisp and the dish is piping hot.

PER SERVING 463 kcals, protein 40g, carbs 54g, fat 11g, sat fat 2g, fibre 5g, sugar 7g, salt 1.31g

Indian potato pie

This is a fail-safe entertaining dish – it looks impressive, the flavour is fantastic, and it tastes great slightly warm or cold, so you can make it well ahead.

TAKES 1 HOUR 35 MINUTES
● **SERVES 6**

700g/1lb 9oz potatoes, sliced
400g/14oz sweet potatoes, sliced
1 onion, chopped
1 tbsp olive oil
1 tsp cumin seeds
2 garlic cloves, crushed
1 red chilli, deseeded and finely
   chopped
1 thumb-size piece ginger, grated
1 tsp each ground cumin, ground
   coriander and garam masala
pinch of dried chilli flakes
200g/7oz frozen peas
juice of 1 lemon
small bunch of coriander, chopped
275g pack filo pastry
25g/1oz butter, melted
½ tsp poppy seeds

1 Bring the potatoes to the boil in a large pan of cold water. Simmer for 5 minutes, add the sweet potatoes and cook for 8 minutes. Drain well, then tip into a bowl.
2 Fry the onion in the oil until soft, add the cumin seeds for 1 minute, then stir in the garlic, chilli and ginger with the rest of the spices. Cook for 2–3 minutes, then stir into the potatoes with the peas, lemon juice and coriander.
3 Heat oven to 190C/170C fan/gas 5. Halve the filo sheets, and use two-thirds, overlapping, to line a 22cm-round loose-bottomed baking tin with a little overhang. Brush each sheet with melted butter and keep the remaining sheets covered. Spoon in the filling and cover with the remaining filo sheets, then fold up the overhanging sides and scrunch up the pastry near the edges.
4 Poke several slits on the pastry top and brush with butter. Sprinkle with poppy seeds. Bake for 40–45 minutes until golden brown, then serve.

PER SERVING 350 kcals, protein 8g, carbs 64g, fat 8g, sat fat 3g, fibre 6g, sugar 7g, salt 0.46g

Spiced pepper pilafs

You can freeze this dish at the end of step 2, but make sure you cool the cooked rice quickly by spreading it out on a baking sheet and leaving it for no longer than 1 hour.

TAKES 1 HOUR • SERVES 8

1 tbsp vegetable oil, plus extra for
    greasing
1 onion, finely chopped
2 garlic cloves, crushed
1cm/½in piece ginger, finely chopped
1 tsp tomato purée
1 tsp ground cumin
1 tsp garam masala
200g/7oz basmati rice
850ml/1½ pints vegetable stock
140g/5oz red split lentils, washed and
    drained
200g bag spinach leaves, chopped
handful of mint leaves, chopped
8 peppers

1 Heat the oil in a large pan with a lid. Add the onion, garlic and ginger, then gently cook for 5 minutes until softened. Stir in the tomato purée and spices, and cook for 1 minute more. Add the rice, stir to coat, then pour in the stock. Bring to the boil, tip in the lentils, cover with the lid and leave to cook over a low heat for 15 minutes, until the lentils and rice are cooked. Stir through the spinach and mint.

2 Heat oven to 200C/180C fan/gas 6. Slice the top off each pepper and reserve. Cut out the middle stalk and scoop out any seeds. Trim the bottoms slightly so they stand upright. Fill each pepper with the rice mix and put the lid on top.

3 Put the peppers on a lightly greased baking sheet and cook for 25–30 minutes or until the peppers have softened. Serve with a green salad.

PER SERVING 209 kcals, protein 8g, carbs 39g, fat 2g, sat fat 1g, fibre 4g, sugar 8g, salt 0.38g

Creamy prawn & spring vegetable pot

Pearl barley is a good source of soluble fibre as well as being rich in valuable minerals, such as calcium, potassium and selenium.

TAKES 40 MINUTES • SERVES 8

850ml/1½ pints low-salt chicken or
    vegetable stock
100g/4oz pearl barley
750g/1lb 10oz new potatoes, sliced
½ spring cabbage, shredded
140g/5oz frozen broad or soya beans
100g/4oz frozen peas
250g/9oz broccoli florets
200g tub crème fraîche
small bunch of dill, chopped
zest of 1 lemon, plus squeeze of juice
600g/1lb 5oz cooked peeled prawns

1 Bring the stock to a simmer in a large frying pan or shallow casserole covered with a lid. Add the pearl barley, cover and cook for 10 minutes. Then add the potatoes and cook, covered, for 12–15 minutes until tender.
2 Remove the lid, increase the heat and bubble the stock for a few minutes to reduce. Stir in the vegetables, crème fraîche, dill, lemon zest and juice. Simmer for 3–4 minutes until the vegetables are just tender.
3 Just before serving, stir in the prawns to heat through and season to taste.

PER SERVING 233 kcals, protein 24g, carbs 31g, fat 2g, sat fat none, fibre 4g, sugar 4g, salt 1.43g

Superhealthy chicken pie

Chicken pie with its creamy filling and crisp pastry is hard to resist. Here it's given a healthy makeover by using filo pastry and packing veg into the creamy sauce.

TAKES 55 MINUTES • SERVES 4

FOR THE FILLING

450ml/16fl oz chicken stock, from
  a cube
100ml/3½fl oz white wine
2 garlic cloves, finely chopped
3 thyme sprigs
1 tarragon sprig, plus 1 tbsp chopped
  leaves
225g/8oz carrots, cut into batons
500g/1lb 2oz boneless skinless chicken
  breasts
225g/8oz leeks, sliced
2 tbsp cornflour, mixed with 2 tbsp
  water
3 tbsp crème fraîche
1 heaped tsp Dijon mustard
1 heaped tbsp chopped parsley

FOR THE TOPPING

70g/2¾oz filo pastry (three 39 × 30cm
  sheets), each sheet cut into 4
1 tbsp rapeseed oil

1 Pour the stock and wine into a frying pan with a lid. Add the garlic, thyme, tarragon sprig and carrots, bring to the boil then simmer for 3 minutes. Add the chicken with some pepper, cover and simmer for 5 minutes. Scatter the leeks over the chicken, cover and simmer for 10 minutes. Remove from the heat and leave on one side for 15 minutes.

2 Strain the stock into a jug – you should have 500ml/18fl oz. Tip the chicken and veg into a 1.5-litre pie dish. Discard the herbs. Pour the stock back into the pan, then slowly pour in the cornflour mix. Boil, stirring, until thick. Remove from the heat. Stir in the crème fraîche, mustard, chopped tarragon and parsley.

3 Heat oven to 200C/180C fan/gas 6. Shred the chicken meat. Stir the sauce into the chicken mixture in the dish.

4 Layer the filo on top of the filling, brushing each sheet with oil. Scrunch up the filo and tuck into the dish. Cook on a baking sheet for 25 minutes until golden.

PER SERVING 320 kcals, protein 34g, carbs 22g, fat 10g, sat fat 4g, fibre 3g, sugar 7g, salt 1.37g

Baked trout with fennel, radish & rocket salad

Being rich in healthy omega-3 fats, trout makes a fabulous special meal for two. Ask the fishmonger to scale and gut the fish for you.

TAKES 35 MINUTES, PLUS STANDING
● **SERVES 2**

2 whole trout, scaled and gutted
½ bunch thyme
2 lemons, 1 sliced, 1 juiced
2 tbsp olive oil, plus extra to drizzle
1 large fennel bulb, finely sliced
100g/4oz radishes, finely sliced
1 tbsp capers, chopped
large handful of rocket leaves

1 Heat oven to 200C/180C fan/gas 6. Slash the trout's skin three times on both sides, then stuff a thyme sprig into each cut. Lay the fish on a baking sheet and fill the cavity with the lemon slices and remaining thyme sprigs. Season the fish, drizzle over some olive oil then bake it for 15–20 minutes until cooked through.

2 Meanwhile, mix the lemon juice with the 2 tablespoons of olive oil, then pour the dressing over the fennel and allow it to stand for 10 minutes. Stir in the radishes and capers, and season. Mix the rocket through the fennel and radish salad. You can serve the trout whole or flake the flesh into large chunks, and serve with the salad.

PER SERVING 465 kcals, protein 57g, carbs 6g, fat 24g, sat fat 4g, fibre 4g, sugar 5g, salt 0.91g

Venison steak with port sauce

A rich, dark red meat, venison is a good low-fat alternative to beef. Still considered a luxury, it's actually very good value and widely available.

TAKES 40 MINUTES ● SERVES 4

750g/1lb 10oz small potatoes, halved or quartered if some are large
2 tbsp olive oil
4 venison steaks
1 tbsp cracked black pepper
chopped parsley, to garnish
peas, to serve (optional)

FOR THE SAUCE

zest of 1 orange, removed in strips, plus its juice
6 tbsp redcurrant jelly
4 tbsp port
1 cinnamon stick

1 Make the sauce by simmering all the ingredients together until the redcurrant jelly has completely melted. Keep warm.

2 Steam or simmer the potatoes until just tender, about 8 minutes, then drain well and add a few drops of oil. Keep warm until ready to serve.

3 Lay the venison on a board. Sprinkle some of the black pepper and a little salt on each side, pressing the pepper into the steaks. Heat the remaining oil in a pan. When it has a shimmering surface, add the steaks, two at a time. Cook for 2 minutes on each side for rare steaks, 3 minutes for medium and 4 minutes for well done. When cooked, return all the steaks to the pan and pour over as much of the sauce as you wish. Warm through for 1 minute then sprinkle with the parsley. Serve with the potatoes and peas, if you like, and any extra sauce spooned over.

PER SERVING 460 kcals, protein 37g, carbs 48g, fat 14g, sat fat 2g, fibre 2g, sugar 20g, salt 0.27g

Pork tenderloin with chipotle sauce & pickled red onions

Blackening the garlic adds a smoky flavour to the spicy sauce. Serve the sauce, onions, pork and tortillas separately so people can help themselves.

TAKES 55 MINUTES • SERVES 4

2 red onions, one thinly and one thickly sliced
juice of 2 limes
2 tsp dried oregano
8 fat garlic cloves, unpeeled
6 medium plum tomatoes, halved
2 tbsp chipotle paste
2 tbsp chilli powder
3 tbsp brown soft sugar
2 pork tenderloins, about 500g/1lb 2oz each
coriander sprigs and warm soft tortillas (flour or corn), to serve

1 Put the thinly sliced onion in a bowl with the juice of 1 lime, half the oregano and a pinch each of salt and pepper. Set aside.

2 Dry-fry the whole garlic cloves in a non-stick pan until blackened on both sides, about 8 minutes, then peel. Heat the grill. Arrange the thickly sliced onion on a baking sheet with the tomatoes, cut-side up. Season and grill until blackened, about 8 minutes. Tip into a bowl with 1 teaspoon of the chilli powder, 1 tablespoon of the sugar, the garlic, chipotle paste, and the remaining lime juice. Season and whizz in a blender until smooth. Heat through in a pan.

3 Rub the pork with the remaining chilli powder, oregano, sugar and some seasoning. Grill for 5 minutes each side until cooked. Serve sliced in warm tortillas with some sauce, the onion mixture and coriander.

PER SERVING 305 kcals, protein 31g, carbs 25g, fat 10g, sat fat 3g, fibre 3g, sugar 20g, salt 0.53g

Marinated lamb steaks with barley salad

Barley has a low GI, so it will leave you feeling fuller for longer. This recipe is high in fibre and a good source of iron, and it counts as two of your 5-a-day.

TAKES 45 MINUTES, PLUS MARINATING
● SERVES 2

2 tbsp olive oil
2 garlic cloves, finely chopped
pinch of dried chilli flakes
small bunch of mint, chopped
2 lean lamb leg steaks (about 100g/4oz each), trimmed of any fat
100g/4oz pearl barley
200g/7oz broad beans, fresh or frozen, podded and skins removed, if you like
100g/4oz frozen petits pois
1 small red onion, finely chopped
zest and juice of 1 lemon

1 Mix together 1 tablespoon of the oil, the garlic, chilli, half the mint and some salt and pepper. Rub all over the steaks, then if you have time, leave to marinate for up to 2 hours.

2 Cook the pearl barley in boiling salted water until tender, but not too soft, about 20 minutes. Cook the beans and peas in the same pan for the last 2 minutes. Drain really well, then tip into a large bowl. Add the red onion, remaining mint, lemon zest and juice, remaining oil and some salt and pepper. Toss everything together.

3 Heat a griddle or frying pan until almost smoking and cook the lamb for 4 minutes on each side for pink, or longer if you prefer your meat well done. Divide the barley salad between two plates and serve with the sliced grilled lamb, drizzled with any pan juices.

PER SERVING 522 kcals, protein 33g, carbs 57g, fat 20g, sat fat 4g, fibre 9g, sugar 5g, salt 0.14g

Jerk-chicken kebabs with mango salsa

The cooling fruity salsa makes a lovely contrast to the mild spiciness of the chicken.
A great summer idea for a long, lazy lunch in the garden.

TAKES 40 MINUTES, PLUS
MARINATING • SERVES 4

2 tsp jerk seasoning
1 tbsp olive oil
juice of 1 lime
4 boneless skinless chicken breasts,
    chopped into chunks
1 large yellow pepper, deseeded and
    cut into 2cm/¾in cubes
100g bag rocket leaves

FOR THE SALSA

320g pack fresh mango chunks, diced
1 large red pepper, deseeded and diced
bunch of spring onions, finely chopped
1 red chilli, deseeded and chopped
    (optional)

1 Mix together the jerk seasoning, olive oil and lime juice. Toss the chicken in it and leave to marinate in the fridge for at least 20 minutes or up to 24 hours.
2 Make the salsa by mixing all the salsa ingredients together with some seasoning – add the chopped red chilli if you like extra heat.
3 Heat the grill or barbecue to medium. Thread the chicken onto eight metal skewers divided by the yellow peppers – aim for three of each per skewer. Cook for 8 minutes each side until cooked through and lightly charred. Serve with the salsa and rocket leaves.

PER SERVING 263 kcals, protein 37g, carbs 19g, fat 5g, sat fat 1g, fibre 4g, sugar 17g, salt 0.30g

Breadcrumbed pork with aubergine & spicy tomato sauce

If you can't find pork escalopes choose lean slices of pork fillet and bat them out with a rolling pin. This tomato sauce has a lovely chilli kick.

TAKES 40 MINUTES • SERVES 2

4 pork escalopes, about 100g/4oz each
1 egg white
3 tbsp dry breadcrumbs
400g can chopped tomatoes
1 red chilli, deseeded and thinly sliced
1 garlic clove, thinly sliced
1 tsp sugar
1 large aubergine, cut into 0.5cm/¼in slices
4 tsp olive oil
green beans, to serve (optional)

1 Trim off any visible fat from the pork and season with a little pepper. Beat the egg white with a fork in a shallow dish. Tip the breadcrumbs on to a plate. Coat the pork first in egg, then in breadcrumbs. Chill to set the coating until ready to cook.

2 Tip the tomatoes into a pan with the chilli, garlic and sugar. Bring to the boil, then simmer for about 10 minutes until thickened. Brush the aubergine slices lightly on both sides with a little of the oil. Grill for 3–4 minutes each side until tender and golden.

3 Meanwhile, heat the remaining oil in a large non-stick frying pan. Add the pork and fry for 3–4 minutes each side until golden brown. Serve each pork escalope topped with aubergine slices and a spoonful of tomato sauce, with some green beans on the side, if you like.

PER SERVING 463 kcals, protein 52g, carbs 27g, fat 17g, sat fat 4g, fibre 6g, sugar 13g, salt 0.81g

Maple & star anise roasted plums

You can use one variety of plum for this, or choose a mixture of different colours and flavours. Add the maple syrup to taste – some plums are sweeter than others.

TAKES 50 MINUTES • SERVES 4

700g/1lb 9oz plums, or a mix of plums,
    greengages and mirabelles
juice of 2 large oranges
3 star anise
3–4 tbsp maple syrup
mascarpone or Greek yogurt, to serve

1 Heat oven to 180C/160C fan/gas 4. Arrange the plums in a single layer in a 1-litre gratin dish. Pour over the orange juice and tuck the star anise among the plums. Drizzle over the maple syrup, then gently stir.

2 Bake the plums for 30–35 minutes until the fruit is soft but not collapsed. Serve warm or cold with mascarpone or yogurt on the side. The roasted plums can be kept in the fridge for up to 3 days.

PER SERVING 101 kcals, protein 1g, carbs 25g, fat none, sat fat none, fibre 3g, sugar 24g, salt 0.01g

Cherry & raspberry gratin

Make the most of the summer fruits when they're in season. The contrast of sweet vanilla with the tart cherries and raspberries works very well in this healthy pud.

TAKES 25 MINUTES, PLUS INFUSING
- **SERVES 4**

200ml/7fl oz milk
1 vanilla pod, split lengthways
2 eggs, separated
4 tbsp sugar
1 tbsp plain flour
squeeze of lemon juice
300g/10oz stoned cherries
300g/10oz raspberries

1 Heat the milk and vanilla pod in a pan until nearly boiling, then leave to infuse for 10–15 minutes. Whisk together the egg yolks with 2 tablespoons of the sugar until pale and light, then whisk in the flour to make a paste. Whisk in the warm milk. Pour the mixture into a pan, then cook for 3–5 minutes until thick. Pour through a sieve into a large bowl, discarding the vanilla pod. Leave to cool.
2 Whisk the egg whites until stiff peaks form then add the remaining sugar, a little at a time, whisking well between each addition, until the mixture is thick and glossy. Stir the lemon juice into the custard mix. Add a third of the meringue to the custard and stir. Repeat with the remaining meringue.
3 Scatter the fruit into a large, shallow heatproof dish. Put under a medium grill for 3–5 minutes to soften. Spoon over the custard mix then grill for 3 minutes until the topping is golden.

PER SERVING 218 kcals, protein 9g, carbs 33g, fat 6g, sat fat 2g, fibre 3g, sugar 30g, salt 0.22g

Fromage-frais mousse with strawberry sauce

Making this mousse with cooked meringue not only gives you a wonderfully light and airy texture but also means you can serve it to vegetarians as there is no gelatine.

TAKES 25 MINUTES, PLUS CHILLING
● **SERVES 6**

1 large egg white
50g/2oz icing sugar, plus extra 2 tbsp
grated zest of 1 lemon and juice of ½
500g tub low-fat fromage frais
500g/1lb 2oz strawberries

1 Put the egg white into a heatproof bowl with the icing sugar. Set the bowl over a large pan of simmering water and, using a hand or electric whisk, whisk for 5 minutes until the mixture is light, fluffy and holds peaks when the blades are lifted. Remove from the heat, whisk in the lemon zest, then whisk for a further 2 minutes to cool it down.

2 Fold in the fromage frais, then transfer to six glasses or small bowls and chill. Roughly chop half the strawberries and put them in the food processor with the extra 2 tablespoons icing sugar and the lemon juice. Whizz to a purée, then press through a sieve to remove the seeds. Chop the remaining strawberries.

3 Spoon the chopped strawberries over the mousses, then spoon a little purée over each. Chill until ready to serve.

PER SERVING 118 kcals, protein 8g, carbs 23g, fat none, sat fat none, fibre 1g, sugar 23g, salt 0.13g

Frozen strawberry yogurt

This gorgeous easy-make frozen yogurt is intensely fruit and really creamy – all the joy of ice cream, but totally fat-free!

TAKES 10 MINUTES, PLUS FREEZING
- **SERVES 5**

140g/5oz strawberries
½ × 405g can light condensed milk
500g tub 0%-fat Greek yogurt

1 Roughly chop half the strawberries and whizz the rest in a food processor or with a stick blender to a purée.

2 In a big bowl, stir the condensed milk into the puréed strawberries then gently stir in the yogurt until well mixed. Fold through the chopped strawberries.

3 Scrape the mixture into a loaf tin or container, wrap well in cling film or pop on the lid and freeze overnight, until solid. Remove from the freezer about 10–15 minutes before you want to serve. Can be frozen for up to 1 month.

PER SERVING 173 kcals, protein 14g, carbs 31g, fat none, sat fat none, fibre 1g, sugar 30g, salt 0.34g

Mango & passion fruit ice

This refreshing dessert is as easy as making ice cubes and impressive enough to round off a dinner party. Plus there's the bonus of it providing three of your 5-a-day.

TAKES 15 MINUTES, PLUS FREEZING
- **SERVES 4**

1 litre carton mango & passion fruit smoothie
4 passion fruits, halved
1 mango, peeled, stoned and sliced

1 Pour the smoothie into a container such as a loaf tin and freeze overnight, or until solid. Remove from the freezer and allow to soften slightly for 10–15 minutes. Cut the passion fruit into halves and scrape out the seeds from inside. Set aside.

2 Scoop the frozen smoothie into rough balls using an ice-cream scoop or spoon, then put inside each halved passion fruit. Serve with the sliced mango and passion fruit seeds.

PER SERVING 192 kcals, protein 2g, carbs 47g, fat 1g, sat fat none, fibre 9g, sugar 41g, salt 0.02g

Nectarine & pistachio crunch layers

Use whichever fruits are in season for this pud. Summer berries and hazelnuts are a good combo. Assemble in pretty glasses just before serving.

TAKES 25 MINUTES • SERVES 6

50g/2oz fresh wholemeal breadcrumbs
25g/1oz porridge oats
50g/2oz demerara sugar
25g/1oz shelled pistachio nuts, finely chopped
500g pot fresh low-fat custard
500g pot 0% fat Greek yogurt
2 tbsp maple syrup or clear Greek honey
4 ripe nectarines, stoned, thinly sliced

1 Heat oven to 180C/160C fan/gas 4. Mix the breadcrumbs, porridge oats, sugar and pistachios together and spread out in an even layer on a parchment-lined baking sheet. Bake for 8 minutes, stirring halfway, until crisp and golden brown. Cool.

2 Gradually beat the custard into the yogurt in a mixing bowl. Sweeten with the syrup or honey. Using dessert glasses or pots, layer up the pistachio crumbs, the nectarines and the custard mixture and serve immediately.

PER SERVING 252 kcals, protein 15g, carbs 42g, fat 4g, sat fat 1g, fibre 2g, sugar 31g, salt 0.35g

Apricot & raspberry tart

Filo pastry is a low-fat alternative to richer pastries such as shortcrust or puff.
However, it needs to be brushed with a little fat as it is layered up, to add flavour.

TAKES 40 MINUTES • SERVES 4

3 large sheets filo pastry (or 6 small)
2 tbsp butter, melted
3 tbsp apricot conserve
6 ripe apricots, stoned and roughly
  sliced
85g/3oz raspberries
2 tsp caster sugar

1 Let the filo come to room temperature for about 10 minutes before use. Put a baking sheet into the oven and heat oven to 200C/180C fan/gas 6.
2 Brush each large sheet of filo with melted butter, layer on top of each other, then fold in half so you have a smaller rectangle six layers thick. If using small sheets, just brush with butter and stack them on top of each other. Fold in the edges of the pastry base to make a 2cm/¾in border, then spread the apricot conserve over the pastry sheet inside the border. Carefully slide the pastry base on to the hot baking sheet and bake for 5 minutes.
3 Remove from the oven, arrange the apricots over the tart and brush with any leftover melted butter. Bake for another 10 minutes, then scatter on the raspberries and sprinkle with sugar. Bake for a final 10 minutes until the pastry is golden brown and crisp.

PER SERVING 150 kcals, protein 2g, carbs 22g, fat 7g, sat fat 4g, fibre 2g, sugar 18g, salt 0.33g

Frozen fruit sticks with passion fruit & lime drizzle

These make a light and fruity end to a meal – use your own favourite seasonal fruit – or serve them for a healthy snack, any time of day.

TAKES 20 MINUTES, PLUS FREEZING
- **MAKES 8**

100g/4oz strawberries, hulled and halved
8 seedless grapes
100g/4oz mango chunks
100g/4oz melon chunks
2 kiwi fruits, peeled and cut into chunks
100g/4oz pineapple chunks

FOR THE DRIZZLE
juice of 2 limes
4 passion fruit, halved and seeds scraped out
1 tsp icing sugar

1 Mix the drizzle ingredients in a small bowl, stirring until the sugar has dissolved. If you want the sauce to be smooth, pass it through a sieve to remove the seeds, but you can leave them in, if you prefer.

2 Skewer the fruits on to wooden skewers and drizzle the sauce over, reserving a little for dipping. Pop the skewers in the freezer for 45 minutes, until just starting to freeze. Serve with the leftover drizzle.

PER SKEWER 31 kcals, protein 1g, carbs 7g, fat none, sat fat none, fibre 1g, sugar 7g, salt 0.01g

Yogurt parfaits with crushed strawberries & amaretti

With its thick texture, Greek yogurt is the perfect base for a quick pudding. You can use any mashed or chopped fruit, but end-of-summer strawberries are ideal.

TAKES 10 MINUTES • SERVES 6

400g punnet strawberries, chopped
4 tbsp caster sugar
500g pot low-fat Greek yogurt
12 small amaretti biscuits, crushed

1 In a small bowl, mix the strawberries with half the sugar, then roughly mash them with a fork so they are juicy.
2 Mix the remaining sugar into the yogurt, then layer up the yogurt with the amaretti biscuits and strawberries in six pretty serving glasses.

PER SERVING 182 kcals, protein 6g, carbs 29g, fat 5g, sat fat 3g, fibre 1g, sugar 22g, salt 0.31g

Apple pie samosas

This sweet version of a savoury favourite makes a tempting hand-held family pud.
Try other fruits when in season and serve with low-fat yogurt for dipping.

TAKES 45 MINUTES • SERVES 4

2 cooking apples, peeled, cored and
  chopped
50g/2oz caster sugar
1 tsp ground mixed spice
50g/2oz sultanas
4 sheets filo pastry
25g/1oz low-fat spread, melted
low-fat yogurt, to serve

1 Heat oven to 200C/180C fan/gas 6.
Put the apples, sugar, mixed spice and
sultanas in a pan with 2 tablespoons
water and cook, covered, for 6 minutes
or until the apples are soft, stirring once
or twice. Tip into a shallow dish and
spread out to cool slightly.

2 Cut the sheets of filo in thirds
lengthways, then brush lightly with the
melted spread. Put a spoonful of the
apple filling at the top of each strip, then
fold over and over to form triangular
parcels. Put on a baking sheet and bake
for 15–20 minutes until crisp and golden.
Serve with a dollop of low-fat yogurt, if
you like.

PER SERVING 196 kcals, protein 2g, carbs 42g,
fat 3g, sat fat 1g, fibre 2g, sugar 31g, salt 0.58g

Clementine & prosecco jellies

These glamorous and refreshingly light jellies will add sparkle to any get-together. They can be made and chilled for up to 48 hours before serving.

TAKES 22 MINUTES, PLUS CHILLING
- **SERVES 6**

7 leaves gelatine
600ml/1 pint clementine juice (from about 14 clementines)
300ml/½ pint prosecco
1 sheet edible gold leaf

1 Put the gelatine leaves into a bowl of cold water to soften for a few minutes. Put 100ml/3½fl oz of the clementine juice into a small pan and gently heat. When the gelatine feels soft and the juice is just simmering, remove the juice from the heat and squeeze out any excess water from the gelatine sheets. Drop the sheets into the hot juice and swirl to melt. Make sure there are no visible lumps of gelatine before you move on to the next stage.

2 Stir the hot juice into the rest of the juice along with the prosecco, then transfer the mixture to a jug. Pour out among six small decorative glasses. Sit the jellies in a small tray or dish, cover with a sheet of cling film and chill for at least 4 hours (or up to 48 hours) until set.

3 When ready to serve, use a pair of tweezers to carefully put a piece of gold leaf on the surface of each jelly.

PER SERVING 115 kcals, protein 7g, carbs 13g, fat none, sat fat none, fibre none, sugar 13g, salt 0.07g

Zesty strawberries with Cointreau

If you're making this dessert for children, mix the juice from the zested orange with the strawberries and sugar. Simply splash Cointreau over the adult portions to serve.

TAKES 5 MINUTES, PLUS SOAKING

● **SERVES 4**

500g/1lb 2oz strawberries, hulled and halved or quartered, depending on size

3 tbsp Cointreau

zest of 1 orange

4 tbsp icing sugar

mint leaves, roughly torn, to decorate

1 Tip the strawberries into a large bowl. Splash over the Cointreau, add the orange zest and sift in the icing sugar, then give everything a really good mix. Cover the bowl, then leave for 1 hour or more for the juices to become syrupy and the strawberries to soak up some of the alcohol.

2 To serve, scatter the mint leaves over the strawberries and give them one more good stir, then spoon into four individual glass dishes.

PER SERVING 69 kcals, protein 1g, carbs 10g, fat none, sat fat none, fibre 1g, sugar 10g, salt 0.02g

Chocolate baked bananas

Totally irresistible – and you can add 25g/1oz mini marshmallows with the chocolate for an even yummier result.

TAKES 35 MINUTES ● SERVES 4

4 ripe bananas
2 × 32g bags chocolate buttons
vanilla ice cream, to serve

1 Heat oven to 200C/180C fan/gas 6, or heat up the barbecue. Make a slit through the skin of the bananas along one side – making sure you don't cut all the way through to the other side. Poke in the chocolate buttons along the cut. Put each banana on to a sheet of foil and crimp the edges together to seal into a parcel. Transfer to a baking sheet and cook for 25 minutes until the bananas have turned black (or pop straight into the barbecue embers for 15 minutes).
2 Serve with a scoop of ice cream and any melted chocolate that has escaped!

PER SERVING 173 kcals, protein 2g, carbs 32g, fat 5g, sat fat 2g, fibre 1g, sugar 30g, salt 0.03g

Index

Also available from BBC Books and *Good Food*

bbegoodfood.com

Great-value family food

Nutty chicken curry

Easy weeknight suppers

Easy sweet & sour chicken

Smart entertaining

Sea bass with sizzled ginger,
chilli & spring onion

Hundreds of desserts

Berry slump

Over 6,000 recipes you can trust